EL EQUIPO MAZZANTI

Inspiration and Process in Architecture

Edited by
Francesca Serrazanetti, Matteo Schubert

Published by Moleskine SpA

Series and Book Editors
Francesca Serrazanetti, Matteo Schubert

Publishing Director
Roberto Di Puma

Graphic design
A+G AchilliGhizzardiAssociati

ISBN 978-88-6293-885-3

Text "Playing architecture. Project concerns
in the work of Giancarlo Mazzanti"
by Hugo Mondragón L.
Text "How to Make a Mazzantic Park"
by Ciro Najle
Other texts by Francesca Serrazanetti

Moleskine© is a registered trademark

First edition April 2017
Printed in Italy by Galli Thierry

We would like to thank
Mariana Bravo and Carlos Medellin

Inspiration and Process in Architecture is a series of monographs on key figures in modern
and contemporary architecture. It offers a reading of the practice of design which emphasises
the value of freehand drawing as part of the creative process. Each volume provides a different
perspective, revealing secrets and insights and showing the various observation techniques
languages, characters, forms and means of communication.

Contents

Toys and architectural diagrams

Writings

A space of relationships for performative architecture

The architecture of Giancarlo Mazzanti is based on relationships in at two least ways. Firstly, because it stems from the conviction that it is the result of a collective and inclusive effort, involving the various figures involved. And, secondly, because it creates spaces open to the people's action, and finds fulfilment only through the encounter with them.

If the first point is part of a trend towards participation with roots firmly established, above all in the history of European architecture, and which is bound up with a profoundly social and political approach, the second is receptive to guidelines related to a way of conceiving architecture as a continuous process, an 'open work' in which the relation between the space and its users is continuous and indissoluble.

This is particularly evident in the installation designs devised by El Equipo Mazzanti for certain exhibitions: participation in events like the Chicago Biennial, the Venice Biennale and the Milan Triennale was treated as an opportunity to declare that architecture can be, in practice, a space of relationship. And, by exploiting the potential for experimenting, condensing a range of experiences into an installation with restricted dimensions, it has shown that the Colombian firm sees architecture as above all a performative space. Performative because it requires direct action by both sides: the work's ability to adapt and stimulate people, and the latter's readiness to penetrate and enact the work itself. Hence, in this performative approach it is hardly surprising that play has a central function: Mazzanti's exhibit installations mentioned above are veritable devices that establish new ways of relating to the public, stimulating participation and creating novel narrative structures. Just as happens in the finished architectures, and

exactly as happens in a game, in which the rules en-
shrine a grid within which the players can move, guiding
their actions and the game's outcome.

Mazzanti's architecture, as he himself states, is therefore
performative rather than representational. And, just as
happened in twentieth-century theatre, he tries to break
down the 'fourth wall' separating stage from audience,
inventing new practices and departing from established
working methods. This experimental character makes
it especially interesting to look at the instruments and
actions concealed behind the process of work. Not only
sketches and models, but also games capable of re-
counting the compositional (and naturally playful) principles underlying the design practice proper. The games
synthesize, with great immediacy, the heart of the project, the principle that generated it and the criteria that
control its potential for growth. These instruments and
considerations give rise to diagrammatic systems that
function on highly specific principles, while creating the
possibility of realizing multiple projects.

The variety of these compositional and representative
instruments is transversely attributable to all Equipo
projects, grouped in this book by different categories,
each of which focuses on one of the factors guiding the
practice's work. 'Atmospheres and environments' places the emphasis on the performative character of Mazzanti's architecture and on the care devoted to the relation between space and the body. 'Play' shows how the
projects can be seen as aggregates of elements, rules
and openness to meaning. 'Modules and bands' shows
the architecture conceived as open-ended structures,
which can change and develop over time and through
relations with people. 'Growth models' are systems that,
by keeping pieces and elements together, enable projects to take root and then grow like trees. Lastly, the
category 'Landscapes, topographies and geographies'
displays the urge to create not so much individual build-

ings as landscapes capable of forming varied connections between places and their inhabitants.

In this way architecture is an instrument of social inclusion, but it is also action, and its specific objective seems to be to multiply relationships, taking root in the society in which it is built. In this respect it becomes an educational mechanism and a performative device. Just as Cedric Price contended, it encourages people to imagine the unthinkable, fosters social, spatial and environmental exchanges, favours complexity, enhances contradiction, requires attentive users and involvies the observer. All this starting from the creative process.

Playing architecture. Project concerns in the work of Giancarlo Mazzanti

Hugo Mondragón L.

Homo-Ludens. It is difficult to find a more precise expression to define the personality of Giancarlo Mazzanti. In fact, rather than conceiving architecture, he plays it. But it is not a game played without a concern for all the relevant factors. On the contrary, whatever the situation, Mazzanti establishes specific rules of the game that define the logic of his projects, but without entirely stripping the random and fortuitous out of the design process.

Mazzanti very likely feels at ease when some of his design strategies bond with those developed by the Russian Formalists, Dadaists and Surrealists, or if they are viewed along with the post CIAM architectural avant-garde. His attitude as an individual creator is post-modern, but his work seems trapped in a socio-cultural context that is still modern, or at least aspires to be.

Unlike its national predecessors, his work is provocatively direct and pragmatic. He received early professional and cultural recognition and does not seem to aspire to a transcendence conceived in metaphysical terms. The irruption of Mazzanti's work into the Colombian setting has changed the order of things, causing a stir and revealing the obsolescence of some of the instruments used by local critics.

1. Break, risk, rebel

One might suppose that, culturally, Colombia is the outcome of a fruitful encounter between the Caribbean spirit – outgoing, colourful, vibrant – and the Andean spirit – introspective, austere, and sober. However, at least in architecture this is not the case. In the mid-twentieth century, Carlos Martínez arrived at the conclusion that Colombian architecture is characterized by austerity and functionality, and he associated Colombian architecture with the Andean spirit alone.

Martínez saw the architectural work as a cultural product, neither artistic nor intellectual. Architecture advanced by an evolutionary impulse and not by the action of the revolution and/or the avant-garde. Martínez did not assimilate the architect's work to that of the artist or intellectual, but the artisan's craft. The architect works patiently on solutions inherited culturally and introduces subtle innovations where appropriate.

From the late 1960s down to the late 90s, Colombian architects were strongly guided by local critics. If they wanted to be published, they not only had to develop a peripheral work of resistance, with a Latin-American colouring, sensitive to urban form, but also to adapt it to the character of Martínez's Colombian architecture.

Despite this Mazzanti has shown himself to be refractory and irreverent to the local critical program. His work is more concerned with formal architectural experimentation, historical discontinuity, and a revolution in its processes. In this respect, his architecture goes against the grain of the local establishment.

As a Colombian, he does not identify himself with the markedly Andean character typical of Colombian architecture and intentionally makes no attempt to place himself on the Latin American cultural market. On the contrary, he fits quite comfortably into an international context in which the concepts of centre and periphery have been thrown into disarray.

It is very likely that Mazzanti as an architect feels closer to the figure of the artist and intellectual, rather than the craftsman. His work is rich in references to the art world and also shows that he is more concerned with invention than perfection. He believes in the value of the individual creator and the ability to produce ruptures and fractures in cultural processes. He believes in architecture's ability to induce certain kinds of behaviour or action.

2. Strategies of the design process

Mazzanti's design procedure and work clearly occupy a position off-centre in the architectural and cultural context from which they emerge. Instead of interpreting it harmonically, they confront and challenge it, with strategies that seem designed to contradict the architectural programme that established critics have sought to defend for years in Colombia.

As a design strategy, Mazzanti uses estrangement or de-contextualization, which consists in taking any object and placing it in another system to which it is extraneous, so giving it a new significance. He uses this strategy to turn a boulder, mountain range or geometric structure of the natural world into the leitmotif of some of his projects.

Moreover his formal and material strategy draws on a certain strand in modern sculpture and through it on the monolithic, abstract, and primitive. He sees designing buildings as if they were outsize sculptures, as a reminder of the fact that architecture is not just a cultural product: it also belongs to the world of art. Yet the issue is even more complex. With the intention of anticipating the relations that the public forms with his works, he seems to make them closer to art installations and neo-avant-garde happenings from the 1960s.

Likewise it is possible to recognize a strategy of expansion of the field in some of Mazzanti's works. This is rooted in allusions to certain topographic elements. The buildings are constructed as if they were mountains. This seems to be inscribed in the tradition of 'Alpine Arckiteckture' and Land Art: designing topographies means designing architecture. Hence architecture is landscape and landscape is architecture.

As a strategy of use and function – essentially a formal strategy – Mazzanti uses open and flexible geometric forms relating to the cluster or tapestry, rather like those devised by Team X. In this way he seeks to cope with the complex web of stresses in an unstable environment and to support significant levels of change in time.

On the other hand, he also has a strategy of atmosphere. In the moderate tropical climate of Colombia it is not possible to consider the image of the building as a comfortable air-conditioned container detached from the exterior. By placing the emphasis on creating inner atmospheres and landscapes rich in fresh air, shade and vegetation, he places his architecture, endowing it with an atmosphere and tropicalizing it.

Finally, Mazzanti uses strategies of seduction. From the study of contemporary popular material culture he realizes that a moderate dose of idiosyncrasy is critical to succeed in seducing the user of his works of public architecture. In an obvious allusion to the concept of the ´people´s palace´, he designs emblematic works, unique, well-rounded and distinct. This sense of the work, articulated in a language accessible to the general public, and set in the midst of fragile physical and social contexts, seems to be the unifying thread that gives a sense of continuity to his work.

3. Architectural and cultural significance
The final concern of this essay is to understand the significance of Giancarlo Mazzanti´s work. As with almost all phenomena, it is significant on a variety of levels.
Mazzanti´s work is accessible. The general public has no difficulty in understanding it, realizing they are faced with an example of ´cultivated´ architecture. In a sense, his work has served to build bridges between the discipline of architecture and the general public, and has enabled his buildings to become elements rich in social and cultural meanings.

Mazzanti's work is rebellious. Just as modern architects rebelled against the authority of the Beaux-Art tradition, or members of Team X rebelled against the orthodoxy of modern architecture, so his work rebels against the programme of Colombian architecture that dominated the local scene for decades, as well as against the functionalism introduced by the industrial revolution.

Mazzanti's work is international. He is not interested in embedding it strictly in a programme of regional implementation. His work has triggered interest around the world and engages in a dialogue with leading figures on the contemporary architectural scene. In this respect it is more centre than periphery.

Mazzanti's work is expansive; he is unable to conceive of any separation between architecture, sculpture and landscape. It relates to modern sculpture but also installations and Land Art. He is much more interested in the logics of change than those of repetition and persistence. Mazzanti's work is tropical. Not in the stylistic sense, but in the way its design approaches the climate. Many of his buildings take advantage of the climatic conditions to be open, airy, and shady. They do not have the defensive attitude adopted by buildings designed for extreme climates; on the contrary they are easy, relaxed, and extroverted.

Finally Mazzanti's work is a game. And like every game it has a content of risk and cautious irresponsibility. Each project defines its own specific rules yet some things remain constant. It is a formal game, governed by geometry. In this sense, the logics of the forms of production lie at the heart of his design concerns, and his project seems to consist of a constant questioning of the capacity of form to define architecture.

How to Make a Mazzantic Park

Ciro Najle

I.

Start by criticizing linear determination as the dominant architectural engine of organizational change. Overcome its addictive dependence on cause-effective relationships and wilful thinking, criticize its inherent enforcement of authorship, smash its idealistic constructs, its heavy-handed symbols, solid icons, grand ideas, and stiff organizations. Unlock its heroic mandates, disengage its ambitious intentions, discredit its ostentatious promises, altogether give up its extravagant temptations, forget its braveness, and unearth the perverse paradox of its achievements.

II.

Continue by denaturalizing and reconfiguring its severe ethics. Reveal the rigid nature of functional segregation, expose the reductive weakness of functional specialization, loosen up the established typologies on which they stand, lay bare the schematic character of induction, question the role of difference, break down objects into smaller workable pieces, and reset a value system based on robustness rather than perfection, on resilience rather than efficiency, on open-endedness rather than finality, on incompleteness rather than perfection, and on pliability rather than flexibility.

III.

Now engage an architectural program. Dismantle the notion of necessity as a self-evident category, dilute its self-imposed seriousness without relaxing its productive pressure, escalate plain need into sheer urgency, uplift deep concerns into extreme situations, switch severity into swiftness, and upgrade morality into action. Turn duties into opportunities, mandates into potentials, errors into freedom, faults into rules, fissures into abilities. Unburden, release, disseminate. Migrate logics of top-down control into practices of detecting, nurturing, enhancing, and amassing power.

IV.

Programs are thus not to be determined and resolutely stipulated, but rather implied and only indirectly specified. Imbalanced situations are not to be diagnosed and judged, as in a medical summary, or solutions endorsed, as by a medical prescription, or symptoms mitigated, as by a specific drug, or causes eliminated, as by an effective technology, a prosthesis or a means for a cure: the programme is not the conventional guideline of solutions to problems but the creative blueprint of potential performances. It is not a scientifically proven instrument, but an alchemical device.

V.

Distrust building totalities and irreducible wholes. They are narrow-minded compounds integrated in conventional types or poignant singularities, their conventions and/or poignancy hiding their deeper representational or metaphorical character, while their performance remains dubious. Part-to-whole seamless integrity is there to be questioned, tested, teased, broken, flipped, made erratic, turned upside down, and defiantly betrayed, with a view to widening its ethical spectrum and enriching performance capabilities. Run the organization consistently against the grain of its form.

VI.

Oversimplify parts, as if abstracting them down to their minimum, crudest version. By the same means, invest them with character, wit, comicality, or even mood. Pieces (not parts) are prolific primitives, figures lacking figuration other than the one resulting from their capability to relate to one another. Pieces are intense generic geometries, abstract characters, both figurines and toys. They match as much as they mismatch. They depend on one another as much as they stand alone, and are singular. Apparently indifferent, disoriented, dumb-and-numb, their relationships dance.

VII.
After the qualitative breakdown of the whole into pieces, manage their relative orientation, their distances, rhythms, adjacencies, and configure varyingly larger sets ranging from the one to the many, yet preventing the formation of distinct larger organizations. Construct logics only to betray them immediately after: avoid compounds, make disparate arrays, inconsistent alignments, agile sequences, volatile mid-scale orders, irregular series, clumsy successions, and gracious sceneries. Feedback the matching attributes embedded in pieces to increase the potential of unevenness.

VIII.
Displace and replace pieces, interchange their roles, extrapolate logics, vary them, commute them. Repeat or proliferate sets but alter the rate of repetition or the ratio of proliferation. Switch rules: disrupt the order and make it unpredictable, and increase the ability of pieces to disappear without disturbing the whole. Reverse the classical idea of harmonic wholes (where everything, nothing more, and nothing less, is absolutely necessary), submitting the parts to such relational stress that the system blurs: nothing remains essential and everything becomes dispensable.

IX.
Wrecked matrix, diluted magma, broken logics, graceful manifold, unfinished set: the whole is not the mechanical sum of its parts, nor does it consist of their full integration in a higher intelligence, nor is it qualitatively more or beyond them. It is rather altogether indifferent: while composed of its parts, it does not need them to sustain itself. Awkward, disharmonic, slippery, even obscure, and yet reducible, additive, cooperative, and organizationally

transparent, the whole is an entity of a completely different nature than its parts: an abstract creature, a nonessential assembly.

X.

In-between, seize odd fissures, sneaky spaces, deceitful continuities, hidden corners, surprising gaps. Appropriate their potential but do not give them spatial status. Do not name them: let they remain unseen, slips away from sheer pattern, and, especially, unexplained. Do not search for, and do not capitalize locally on exceptions, inconsistencies, and disruptions as new rules. Instead, exploit them globally as symptoms of play. Pieces play because there is play between them. Their position is volatile, uncertain, precarious. They are seeds of revolution, invitations to instability.

XI.

Dangerous, harmful looseness, rather than bland, adaptive looseness, awaits and declares change. Loose wholes are not soft forms of order but active ones, hazardous, threatening, alluring traces of what organizations may become. Make the most out of ruggedness without making it predictable. Enhance it, but avoid utter chaos. No trace of completeness, only signs of the possibility of failure. Involvement is activated and maintained by imminence and risk. Order must be retained behind the feel of warning to prolong indefinitely its presence. Instability must remain weak to be such.

XII.

Such form of playfulness is not intuitive, nor subjective, but the result of a carefully staged set of orders and irregularities, whose formally embedded but difficult distribution of relationships creates play between the parts of a whole. These pieces themselves are loaded with character by means of oversimplification, and the whole, accordingly, light-heartedly acquires a character of its own, independent of them. Consequently, play operates as a material construct as precise as rigour. But it is divergent and has a completely different target: engagement, instead of dominance.

XIII.
Furthermore, playfulness has rules: the rules of the play that takes place between the parts of the unstable whole. These rules project themselves as the regulations of a game that happens only imaginarily (reducing second-level rules to actual rules would turn them into prescriptions). Set instructions, but create enough looseness between them and the actual regulations that manage the relationships between the parts. Call this metaphor, but do not fall in the temptation of setting a literal correlation between these two realms: form and performance must remain distinct.

XIV.
The gameness of the whole, then, does not exactly equal the play between its parts, but is rather its expanded apparition in an artistic form. The same happens with architecture's good intentions: too limited in comparison to what they do at a diffuse level. It is the appearance of game (i.e. the apparition of gameness) that calls for playing a game within architecture. This differs radically (and could be understood as its opposite) from following the rules of an architectural system. Do not determine, but insinuate, suggest, and evoke: a material practice, but one that acts indirectly.

XV.
Parts (as pieces) are there exposed, made available, simple and easy to understand. And yet they retain the challenge of how and in how many ways they can be put together, and the enigma of what it is that they actually look like. Similarly, their relationships are clear, but not predictable, often appearing erratic, unexplained, difficult, even unfairly or uncomfortably situated. The whole that results of this is not a congruent construct, but one

that has a life and character of its own, teasing the role and flattening the sense of its parts: such is the paradoxical board of the game.

XVI.
The joyful-system-based totality is a complicated-complex whole where parts, treated as singular yet repetitive or systematically varying dumb-and-numb pieces, are locked to one another without knitting a solid, rigorous, and compact set, thus enabling spatial and material play between them, and therefore nurturing an imaginary global interface, which, far beyond merely enabling the concrete management of performance and/or real participation into its dynamics, appears to create the feel of play. The expression of this interface is the project of architecture, its modality.

XVII.
The particular form of part-whole artfulness involves such modal apparition, which acquires form much before declining into the expression of the severe promise of systemic ubiquity, and far beyond the actuality of systemic adaptability to needs. Ethically entrenched with a larger family of modalities, and yet intrinsically singular and irreducible to them, these modal apparitions, i.e. these projects, claim a territory for architecture that is, at the same time, immediate and aloof, available and intangible, direct and incorporeal, metaphorical and literal, playful and serious.

XVIII.
Only then, bring back the programme (with capital letters). The programme is education, in a broad sense: non-paternalistic, non-prescriptive education, but also non-demagogical, non-idealistic education, both. Education for the sake of it, education as encouraging the pleasure of learning in general, education as absolute consciousness within the radically unconscious realm of play as apparition. The joyful systemic whole is em-

bedded with rules (strictly loose rules that betray themselves) and is itself a paradox of order. That is its motivation as a form, and its performance as content.

XIX.

Joyful systemic wholes and over-simplistic dumb-and-numb pieces: playful form that appears to perform and non-paternalistically educates. The modern program of social transformation takes here the renewed broader form of the non-prescriptive, but it does not decline into yet another form of post-postmodern celebration. The architectural project resuscitates from the oppressive dominance of critique without falling in a newly innocent transformative project. Playfulness is an explicit form of humour: an amusing form beyond cynicism and an earnest form without naiveté.

XX.

Rather than the intellectually comfortable expression of radical scepticism, often misplaced in the critical domain by the same cynical motivation of the scepticism that gives rise to it, these joyful modalities that we here call play as apparition, operate through radical reduction, dumbing down, disruption, displacement, complication, jaggedness, and the diffusion of performance into feel, and work as light-heartedly distorted intensifications of the real, turning responsibilities into desires, tempered behaviour and good intentionality into radical creativity, and systems into games.

XXI.

These games, precisely because of this turn of systems into beings, more than environments, behave as if they were creatures: artificial forms of life with a character of their own, generic and yet singular, ubiquitous and yet discrete, unnatural and yet all the more real. They act and develop character, they adapt to their context while preserving autonomy as self-standing individuals, they break without collapsing, they strive for life and require feedback to perform, they communicate through primitive expressions, they breath and host, welcome, mimic, or reject other beings.

XXII.
Creatures with power, strength, force, mood, and character, rather than environments with dynamics, potential, abilities, ambience, and atmosphere: they project themselves aggressively into the real as modalities of play without an ideological agenda. Far from being transformative by means of a conscious plan, their power lies in the crudeness of their features, in the clandestine space of their fissures, in their enigmatically displaced logics, in their misbehaviour. Their optimism is not severe but cheerful. Their critique is not outside, not above, but in-between architecture.

XXIII.
Lively symbols of a future unknown, light but encouraging icons of an anti-monumental attitude that overwhelms any content with a casual tone, unceremoniously open organizations that turn the problem of organization into a field of assertive actions, these creatures turn the city (and the world, by extension), through the sheer projection of their presence, into a park of nuisances, a park that integrates, not without friction, entertainment and self-indulgence with education and transformation, overcoming the cynicism of the first and the absolutism of the second.

XXIV.
Welcome to Mazzantic Park. You are both the author and the spectator.

Interview with Giancarlo Mazzanti

66 *Could you tell us how the projects in your practice get started? How far is the process important in your work, apart from the finished architecture?*

Our work starts around a table. There are always three or four of us, architects, because we feel it's important to talk 'horizontally'. We believe we need to avoid the architect speaking ex cathedra and handing down a readymade project. Comparing notes and swapping ideas produces a design that we've all put our hands to. The outcome of this process looks not so much like a project as a diagram defining what we've talked about. This composition, put together out of fragments and ideas, enables us to start work on the real project, creating study models that help us further clarify what we want to achieve. For us it's important, first of all, to ask ourselves what processes we want to trigger.

66 *The way you do architecture is strongly influenced by the local conditions you work in and the relations you succeed in building with the project. The involvement of local communities is particularly significant. How does this develop and interact with your design practice proper*

In many cases we try and work with the community, but this is not always the case. The projects are often developed for competitions, so there's no scope for engaging in such processes. But when the conditions are right, we organize the involvement of the inhabitants, while avoiding asking them directly what they want, because the answer would invariably be 'a soccer pitch'. But we do listen to people, trying to understand the most important things they identify with and appreciating their needs.
Sometimes we also involve an artist, Nicolàs Paris, in these activities. At other times we've organized football matches to help start up a dialogue with the most dangerous groups in the neighbourhood. Or we might meet at different tables with specific groups, like women or

young people. At the start, ours is a very verbal method, and it only becomes a project later on. You can't always count on people's involvement, not everyone has the means to understand what we're trying to do. Often a cultural scenario, a vision, is lacking. When we planned the Medellin Library, for instance, at first most members of the community were against it because they felt it was useless or considered it not a priority. But when the work was done and they realized the effect it was having on the region, they were all highly satisfied.

" Were there certain experiences, authors or works that particularly influenced your architecture?

We've certainly been strongly influenced by certain British groups – Team X, Cedric Price, Archigram. We're interested in all kinds of research that works by parts and modules. Right now we're closely focused on the theme of play: we think of architecture as a game made up of pieces that enable you to make something grow one piece at a time. I'm interested in inserting the playful component in a very functional space. On this point we're strongly influenced by the ideas of Michel Foucault, the themes of knowledge, education and utopia. I would urge everyone to read *Discipline and Punish*, a remarkable essay from 1975.

Some contemporary architects I've always looked at with great interest for their ability to create 'performative architectures' are Bernard Tschumi and Rem Koolhaas. I owe lot to the studies of Tschumi's Cross-Programming, to architectural sequences and spaces, the programmes and movements that produce and reinforce these sequences, the processes of alienation and destructuring. Some of our recent installations, like those for the Chicago Biennial, the Milan Triennale and the Venice Biennale, work along these lines. They are architectures where people have the freedom to interact and play.

Finally, there are two masters I owe a lot to in academic terms – Manfredo Tafuri and Aldo Rossi. Like most students in those years in Latin America, they gave me a theoretical frame of reference in my formation. At university they called me Giancarlo Rossi, because I knew his book *The Architecture of the City* by heart. Then his *Scientific Autobiography* taught me to look at the architecture in a new way. It conveyed the value and the bond of time, both chronological and atmospheric. It gave me that idea of architecture in movement so masterfully expressed in the Teatro del Mondo. We tried to apply it to a project for a museum, where all the walls and spaces can be moved and modified by the artists, depending on what they mean to exhibit. And movement brings us back to play. The influence of play has also been reflected in our experience designing various kindergartens. We believe in the importance of giving others an architecture that is an instrument for learning something and a playful culture helps us achieve this purpose.

❝ *A lot of people consider architecture essentially an aesthetic matter, and if it is to be recognized internationally it has to be based on purely formal principles. But in your case the forms are modelled on relations with people, welded to them, and draw their extraordinary social impact from them.*

It all depends on what you succeed in triggering with people. We're interested in understanding what happens within our architecture, we're interested in what happens within the walls when a person enters the building. This is the social role of architecture, to start a sort of happening. If you offer poor people who live in the suburbs the things that other people haven't got in the city, they feel gratified, they think their lives are enhanced, and so they appropriate the projects very strongly. So it is important, before you start your project, to ask yourself what you want to favour, what relationships, and how you want people to appropriate them, so we can be sure something will definitely happen in our buildings. We're concerned that every individual should be able to use a space in different ways and transform it.

The modular and diagrammatic principle on which many of your projects are based tends to ensure a system of open growth. Do you do this so people can alter and reinterpret the projects, or is it a strategy for controlling the project and ensuring it develops properly?

That depends. At the Sports Coliseo in Medellin, for instance, our project grew without our being involved in it. All at once a new element was created. This is what Roland Barthes called the death of the author. I provide the instructions and you're free to go ahead on your own. Over time architects have become rock stars, artists, but now we have to restore our profession to its central role, as a social and cultural mediator. In a region of Colombia we designed thirty modules for child care centres. We invented the system and the rules, and now they're already building the thirty-first. It's a highly social approach. In countries like ours, where there isn't a lot of money, if you invest in a repeatable module you'll not only be able to build a lot more, but you can also start by implementing just a part of the project and then complete it when the money has been found for the rest of the budget. I believe that this approach can safely be exported and adapted to other places. Even in many European outer suburbs, where there are few amenities, you could start by sowing the first seeds.

Then the modular system enables you to devise several different configurations. Each project, thanks to the performative action, always has its specifics, because it's possible to interpret it. This principle of modules is also linked to Japanese Metabolism. It's not just an idea bound up with social values, but a way of thinking about architecture as an open system, one that changes along with society.

In this respect our architecture is also influenced by biology, molecular systems, growth and evolution. Just as a plant grows by parts and responds to external conditions, so architecture can change in response to different pressures.

A work should always be open-ended. This is a very important point about architecture. I've always found the ideas presented by Umberto Eco in his book *The Open Work* extremely useful. Sometimes I get help from the videos we take after completion of our projects. Through this instrument, I try to understand what the users think after passing through them and living in them. I'd like to carry out more closely targeted research. I'd like to have a 'persecutory' eye like the artist Sophie Calle. I'd like to find out how people live in our architecture by following them, videotaping them without their realizing it, because it would enable us to understand whether a project functions or not. Normally the inhabitants of the neighbourhoods where we've built our projects are pleased. They realize our projects regenerate the environment, change their neighbourhood for the better, and offer opportunities that didn't exist before. I want to clarify the fact that dealing with social values, as far as I'm concerned, doesn't just mean devoting yourself to the poor and the outer suburbs. You can carry out a social project in the centre of town. Now, for example, we're planning a theatre and a library in the heart of the city, but the approach is still highly social, because the project turns on the idea that libraries have changed and are no longer places of silence exclusively devoted to reading. So we're thinking about a 'circus library', with a big square, a huge hammock where people can read but mostly socialize, meet and interact around culture. We're deeply committed to studying and understanding what people do in a library or theatre, which by their very nature are social places. To return to the question, architecture should never be a finished work. A project ought to be able to mutate without an architect. Our role requires us to be ready for change. If the users act on our work, it means they needed to, they felt the urge to do it. Architects are far too busy creating finished works.

They get bogged down in the details, when we ought really to be thinking about what we can create, what we can generate by our work.

In a school we built in Medellin, people can sow and arrange the plants that will alter the building's façades, and we don't know how it's going to develop. This is an important aspect of our projects, the unpredictability of social action.

❝ *In this complex process, above consisting of human relationships, what sort of connection is there between the project materials – sketches, drawings, models, your games – and computer drawing, and how do they still manage to retain their significance?*

The drawings, sketches and games, which are really important, exist because they enable us to render and visualize what we're talking about while we're designing around a table. The drawings then inevitably pass through the computer. But, after this phase, the project returns to the table, with new sketches and new diagrams being created. The most important drawings are always the ones that come out of the meetings, while the computer is only a secondary instrument. I'm obsessed with models, we do lots of study models. Some very complex projects require the assistance of the computer, but it should only be an aid. I'm always upset when young people in universities talk about architecture in terms of technology, about 'fast' and/or 'deformable' models. These are concepts that have nothing to do with the profession. Where are the people? Where's the context? Where's the culture? Technology is vital to helping you manage complexity, but it can't replace the idea, objectives and purposes of a project.

El Porvenir Kindergarten
Bogotá, Colombia, 2009
Sketches and plan studies

Drawings

Atmospheres and environments

El Equipo Mazzanti's design practice continuously explores an approach capable of going beyond the sense of sight. Architecture is not just form: rather it is made up of atmospheres. It relates people and environments, and is born of the indissoluble relationship between bodies and the spaces they enact. The firm's architecture seeks to create environmental conditions capable of amplifying perceptions and intensifying the relations between people and nature. The result is a more expressive architecture, in which environments redefine the value of the object and architectural space, understood as a physical construction to be contemplated and observed, making it a system of bodily and environmental sensations based on humidity, warmth, cold and brightness. Hence the space, starting from the more conceptual exhibition projects and continuing all the way to the completed buildings, changes in relation to the body and its possible uses: it becomes a malleable skin, creating atmospheres and environments that can be transformed by human action.

The wall from static to elastic
Exhibition
Architecture as Art,
XXI Triennale Milano,
Pirelli HangarBicocca
Milan, Italy, 2016
Models and sketches

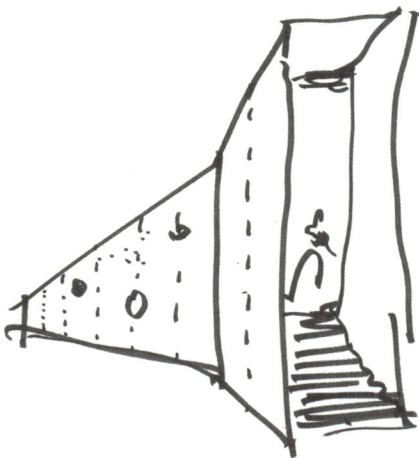

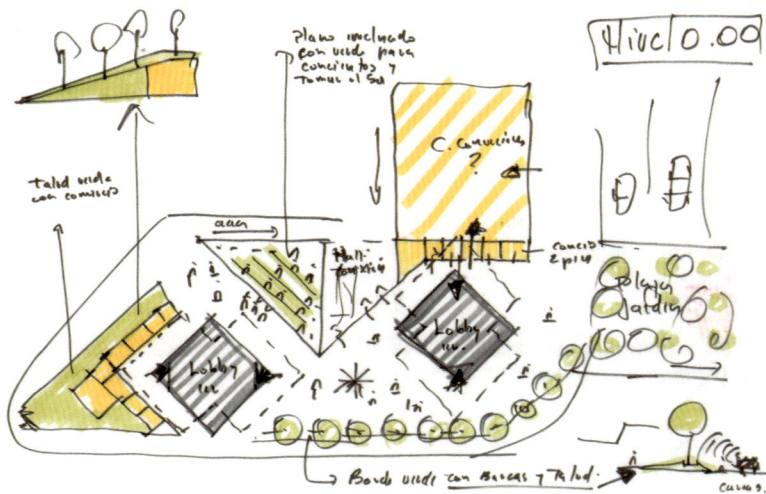

Atrio towers
with RSH+P
Bogotá, Colombia, 2008
Plan studies

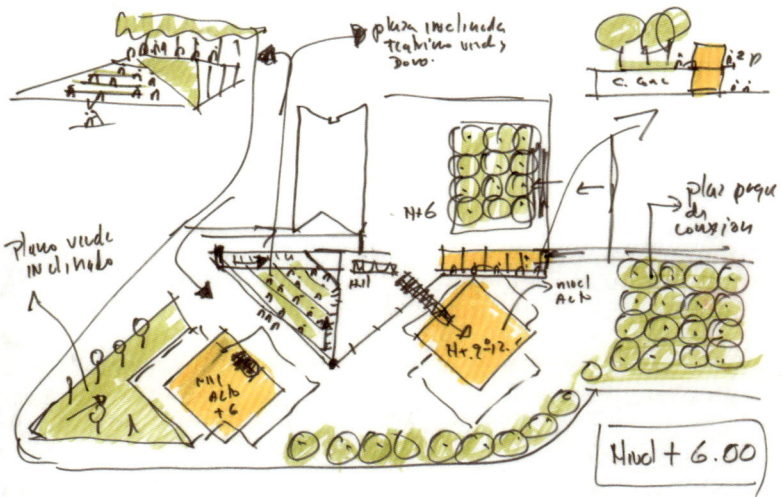

plaza inclinada teatrino verde Dovo.

C. Gac

plan pequ de conxion

Plano verde inclinado

H+6

nivel Alto

H+2=12.

Mivel + 6.00

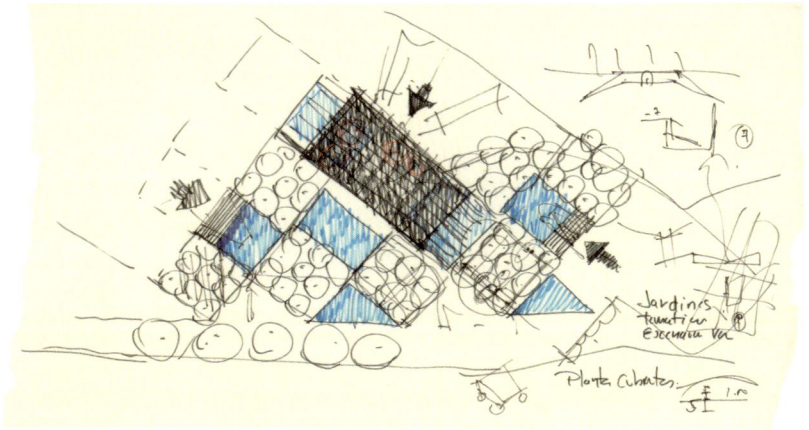

Jardines
temáticos
escuela Var

Planta Cubiertas
5 1:..

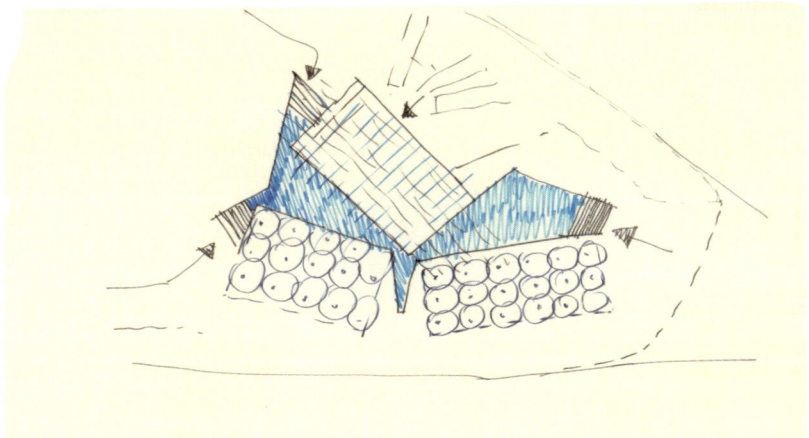

National Memorial Museum Competition
Bogotá, Colombia, 2015
Study sketches and diagrams

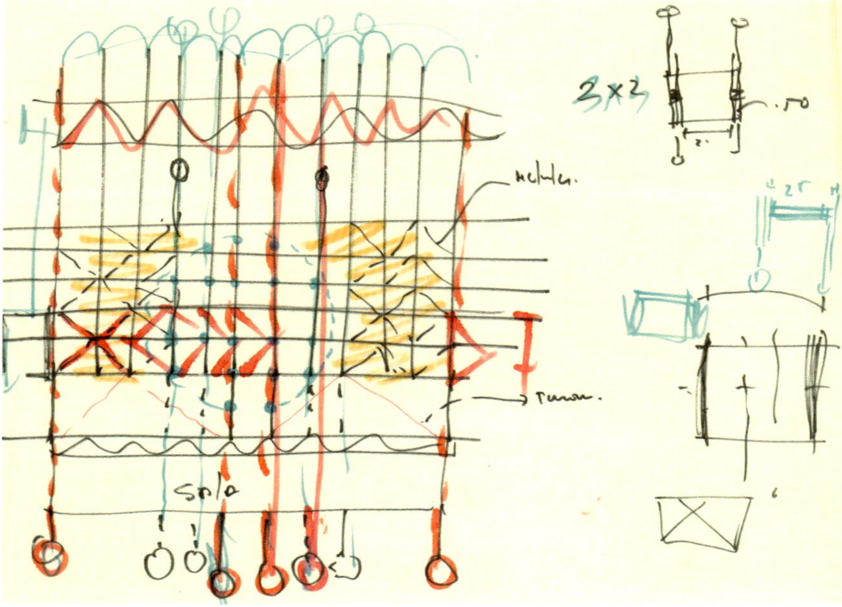

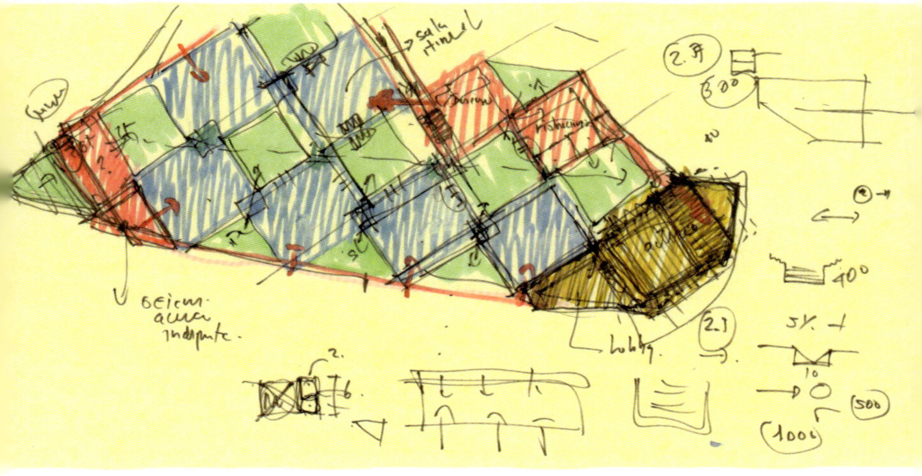

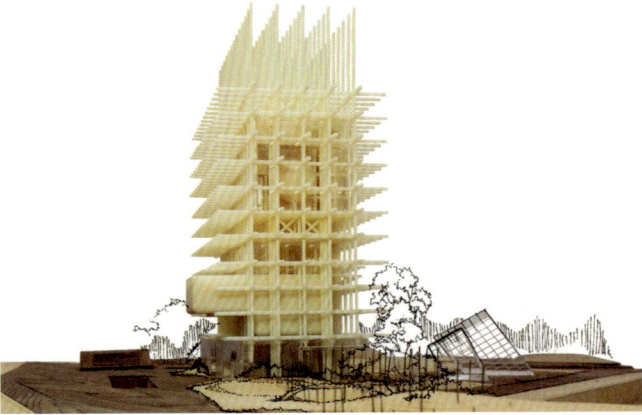

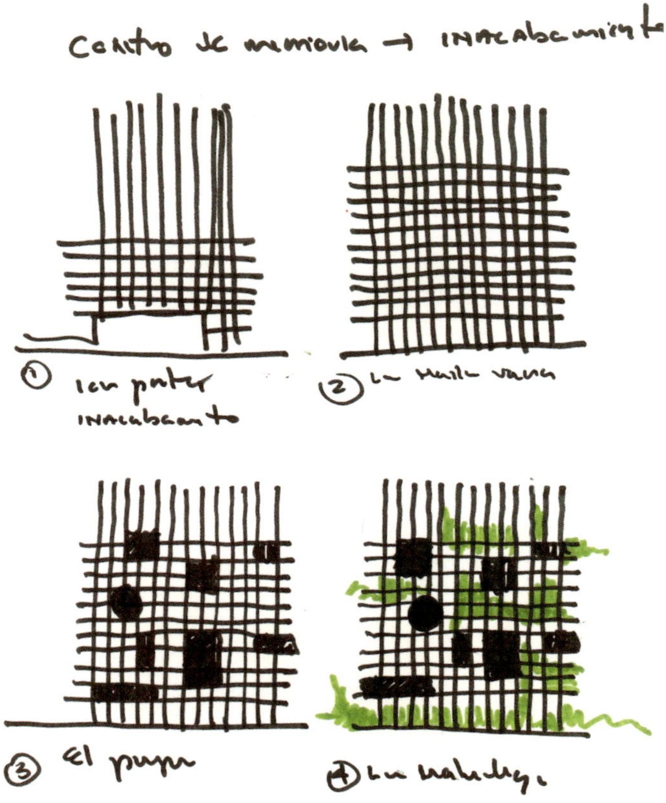

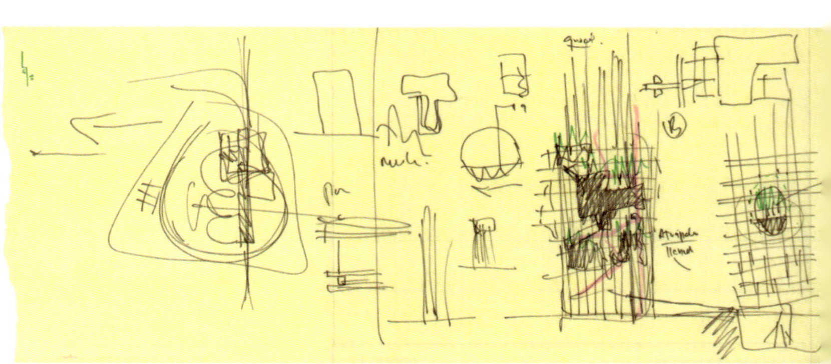

Centro de memoria → inacabamiento

① lan parter
inacabamiento

② la maila varia

③ el pupu

④ la maladiga

**National Memorial
Museum Competition**
Bogotá, Colombia,
2015
From unfinished to
building. Evolution
studies

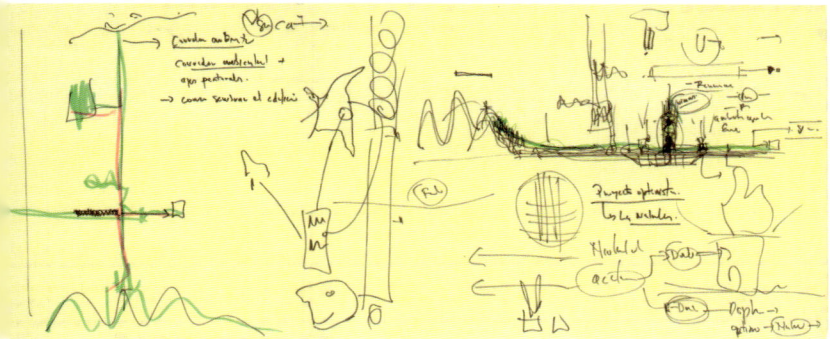

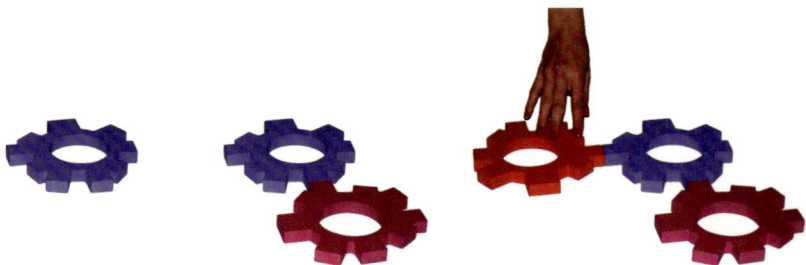

**Loris Malaguzzi
Kindergarten Competition**
Reggio Emilia, Italy, 2012
Toys and sketches

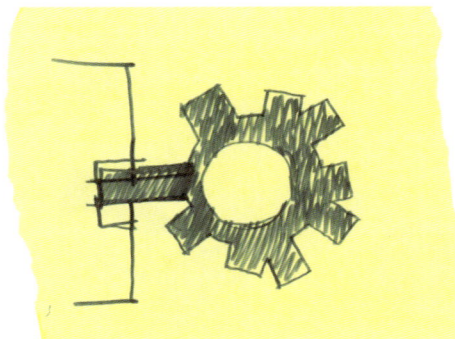

**Loris Malaguzzi
Kindergarten
Competition**
Reggio Emilia,
Italy, 2012
Distribution studies:
from the basic
element to the
composition
of the pieces

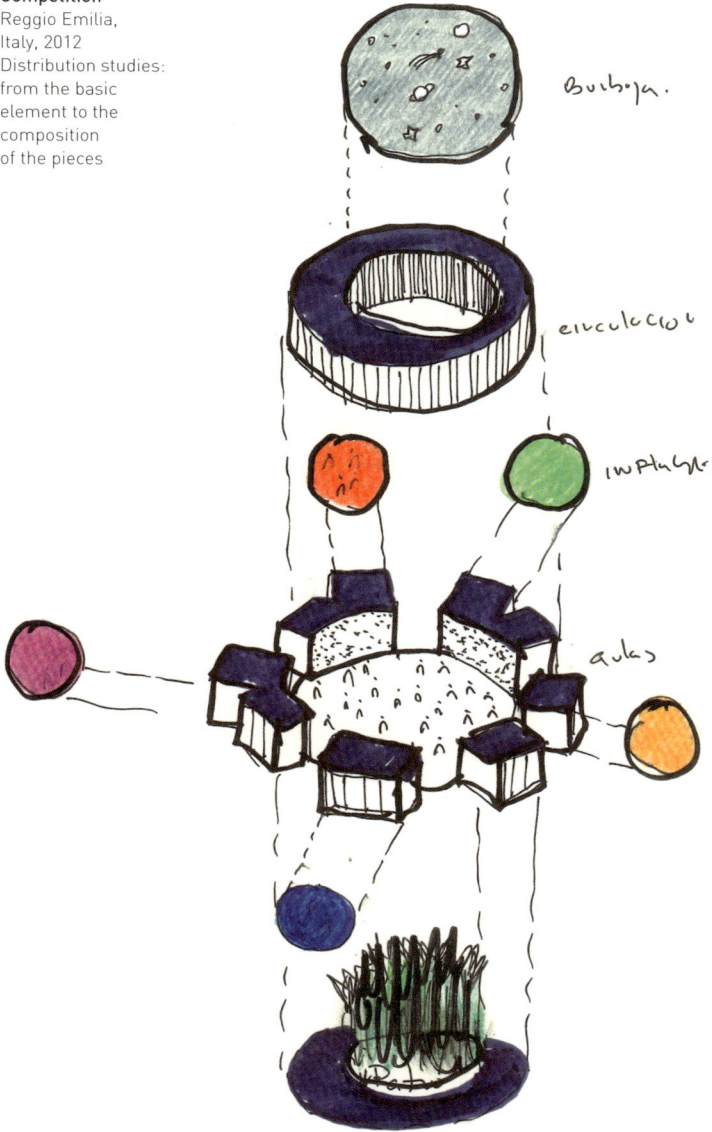

Burbuja.

circulacion

implants

aulas

asilo nido/Baru

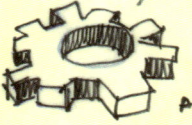

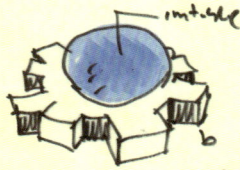

a

imt.ule

b

intelly

c

d

gonfubili.

e.

— un edificio que pudou ambientes pedagogicas
se viste y se disuh

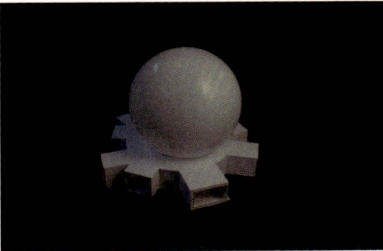

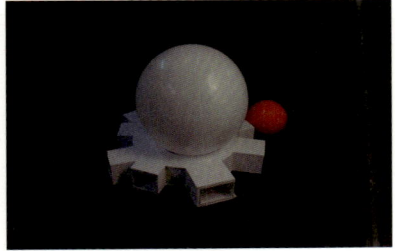

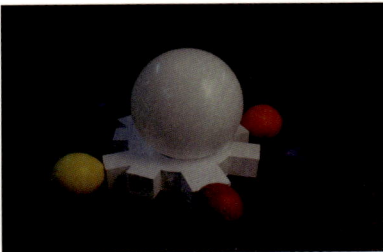

Play

Giancarlo Mazzanti sees architecture as play, in the fullest and most versatile sense of the term. It is something that we enact. It is a space that can be shaped and transformed, and the more it is open to manipulation the more it can be understood by its inhabitants. Play then becomes a device structured by an immediate yet complex set of rules, capable of controlling the evolution of the spatial systems and the interaction between them and people. It is an instrument for composing and communicating the project, presenting it and changing it, based on open-ended systems and relations between the parts. Architecture, like play, is made up of elements that, mixed and reorganized, can function differently within predefined parameters. But for them to enter into action calls for the presence of a person, or better a team, to give a meaning to the composition of the pieces.

these and following pages
IB College Anglo Colombiano
School competition
Bogotá, Colombia, 2014
Toys, model and sketch

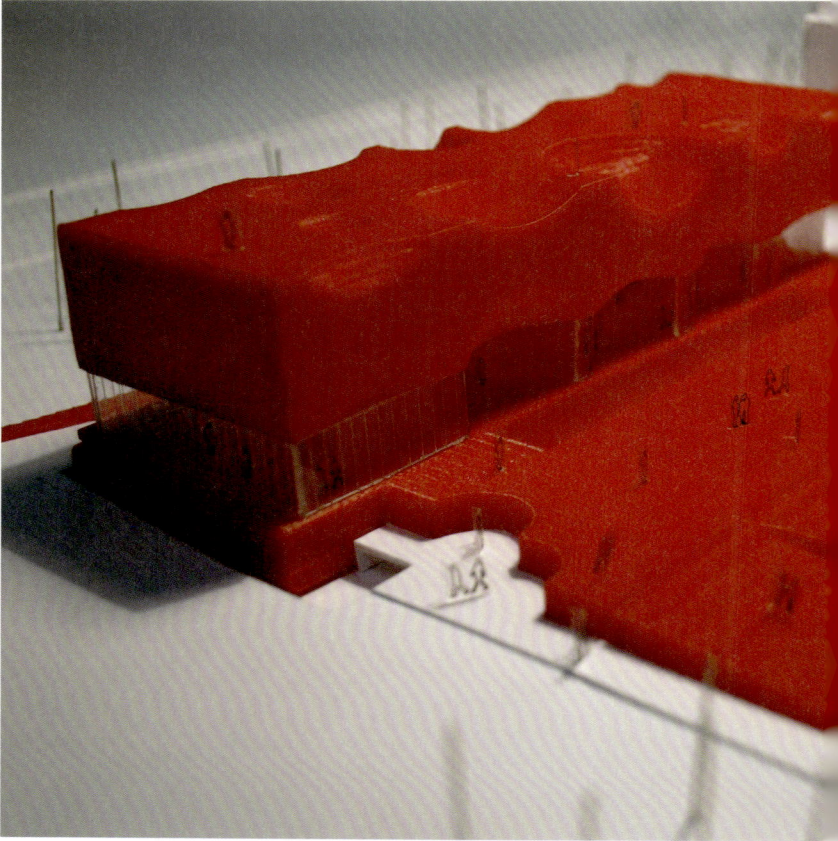

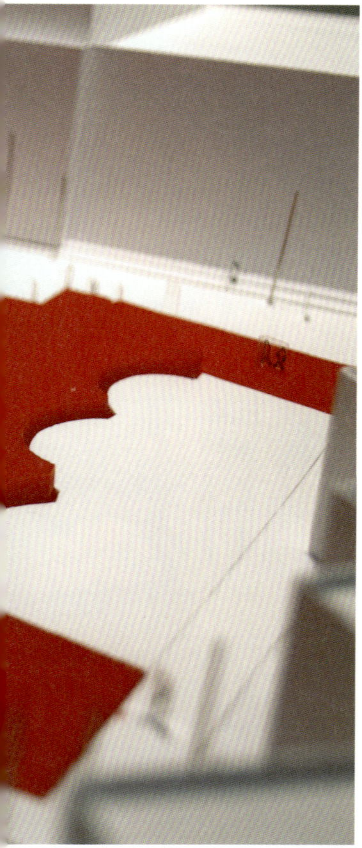

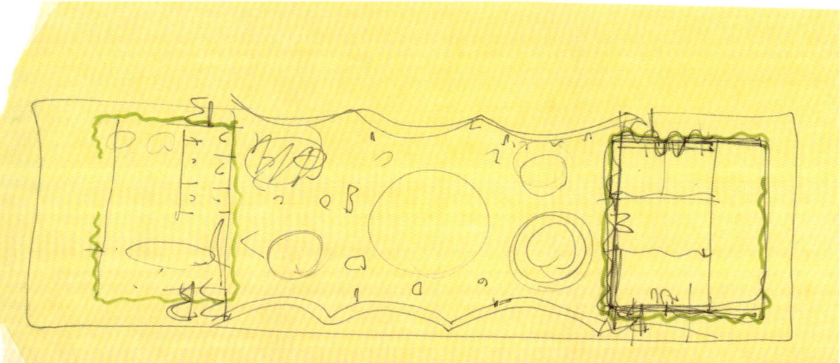

IB College Anglo Colombiano
School competition
Bogotá, Colombia, 2014
Elevation studies

Speaking Architecture
with the artist Nicolás Paris
Exhibition, Chicago Architecture Biennale 2015
Chicago, United States, 2015-2016
Cut and paste exercise

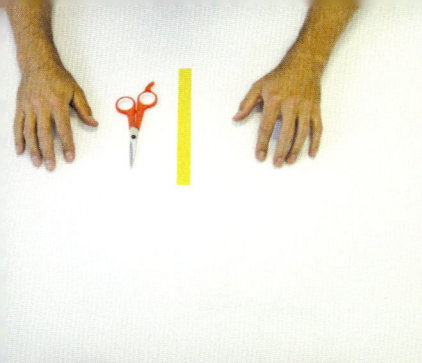

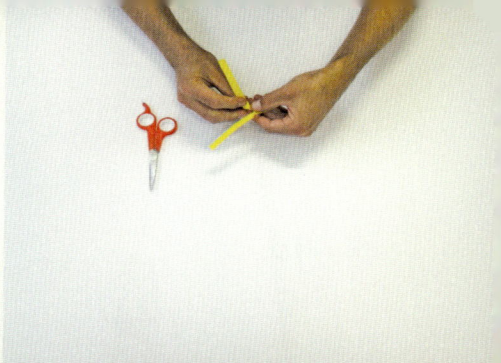

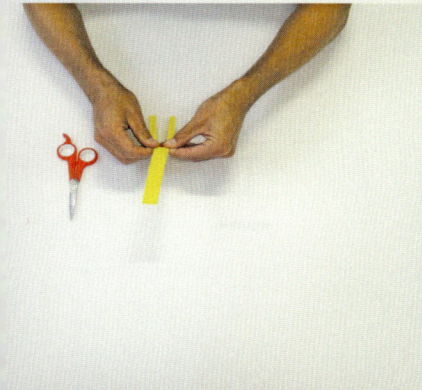

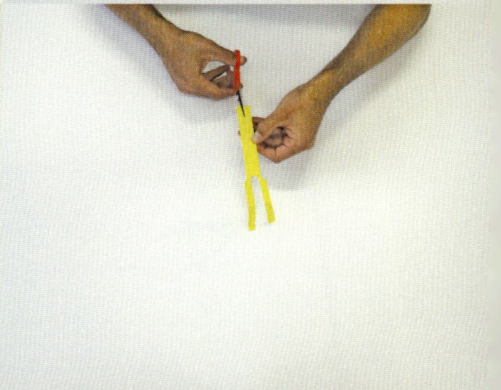

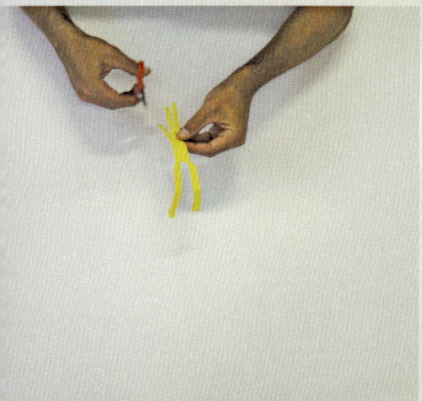

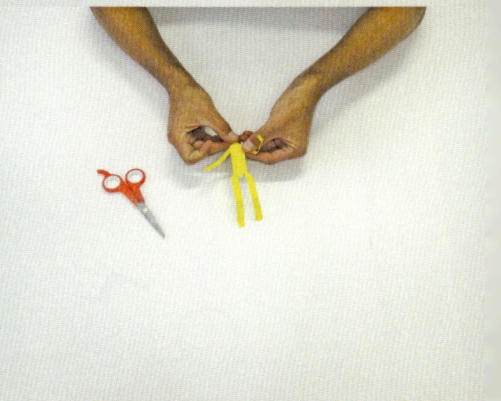

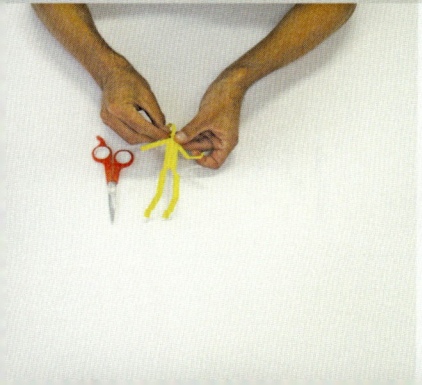

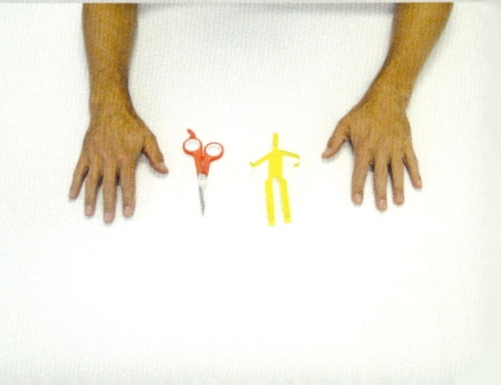

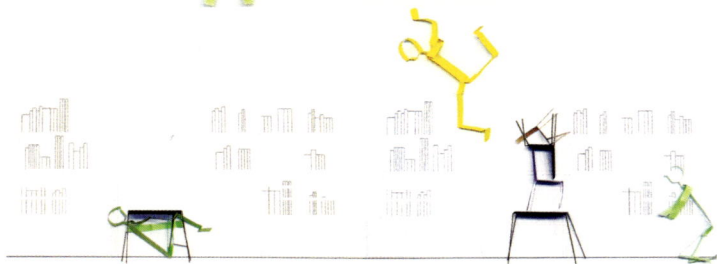

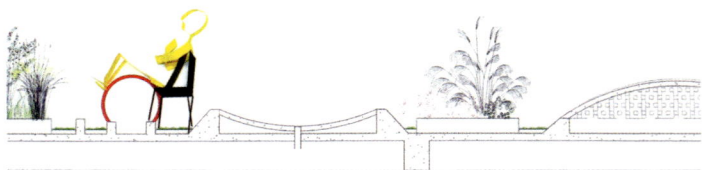

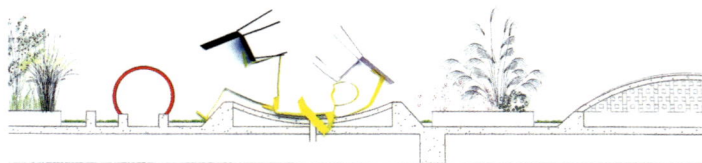

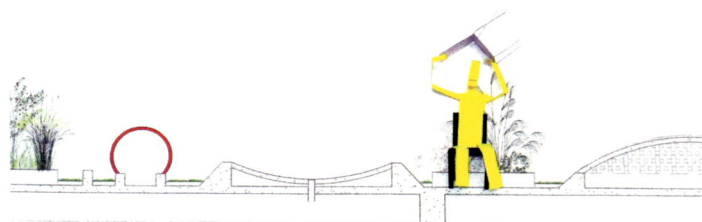

left
Speaking Architecture
with the artist Nicolás Paris
Exhibition, Chicago Architecture Biennale 2015
Chicago, United States, 2015-2016
Collage

right
Trustics
Exhibition, Venice Biennale 2016
Venice, Italy, 2016
Interaction and movement studies

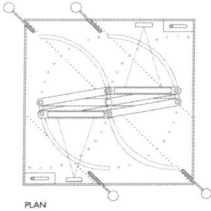

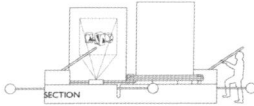

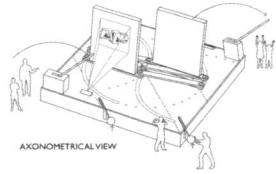

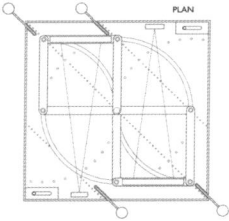

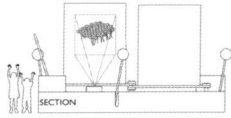

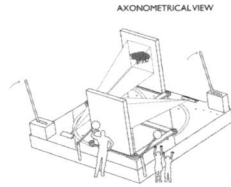

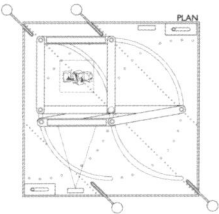

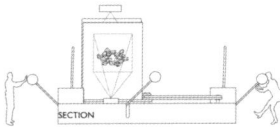

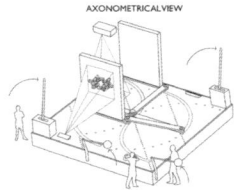

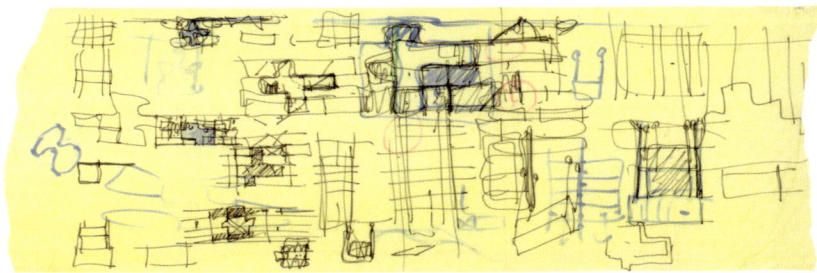

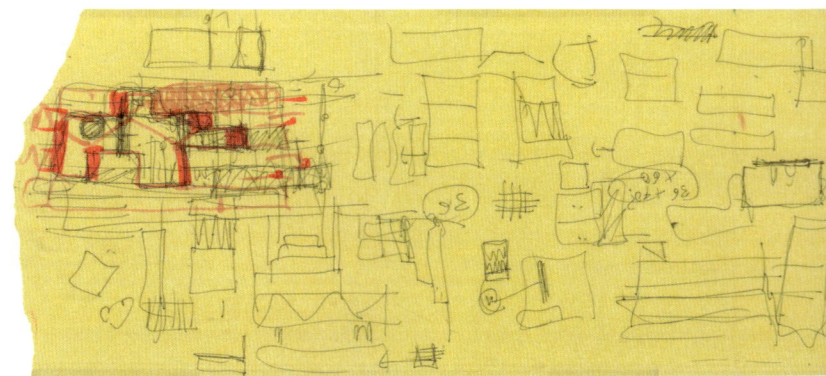

Guggenheim Helsinki Competition
with the artist Nicolás Paris
Helsinki, Finland, 2014
Study sketches and construction-toys

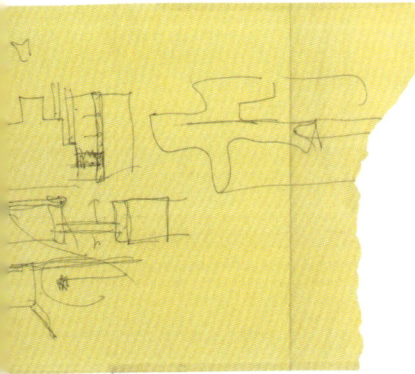
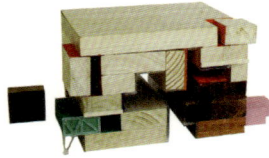

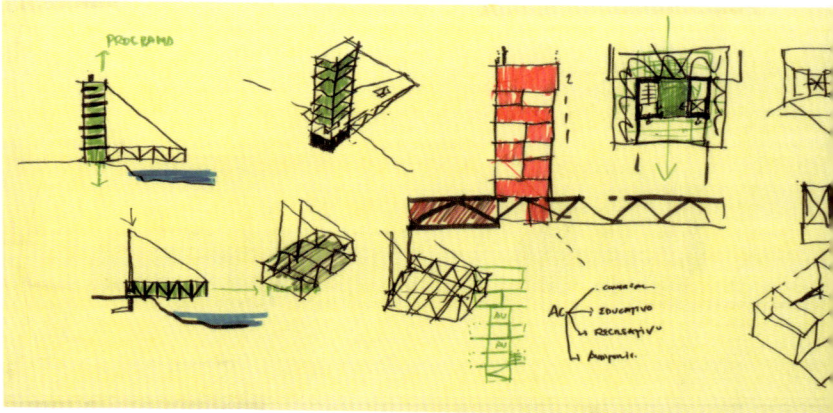

Guggenheim Helsinki Competition
with the artist Nicolás Paris
Helsinki, Finland, 2014
Study sketches

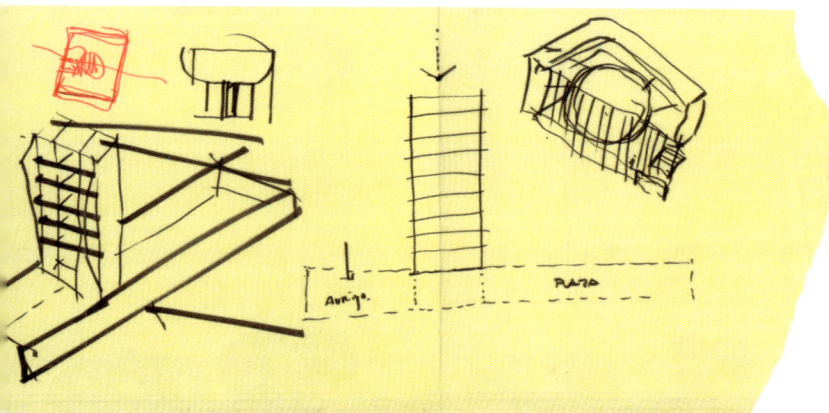

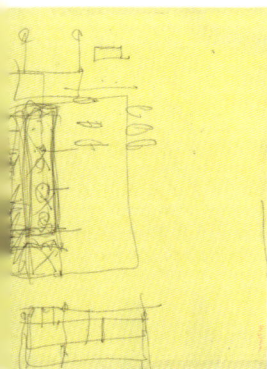

El Porvenir Kindergarten
Bogotá, Colombia, 2009
Toys and study model with sketch

El Porvenir Kindergarten
Bogotá, Colombia, 2009
Sketch, plan study and model

el puvenur

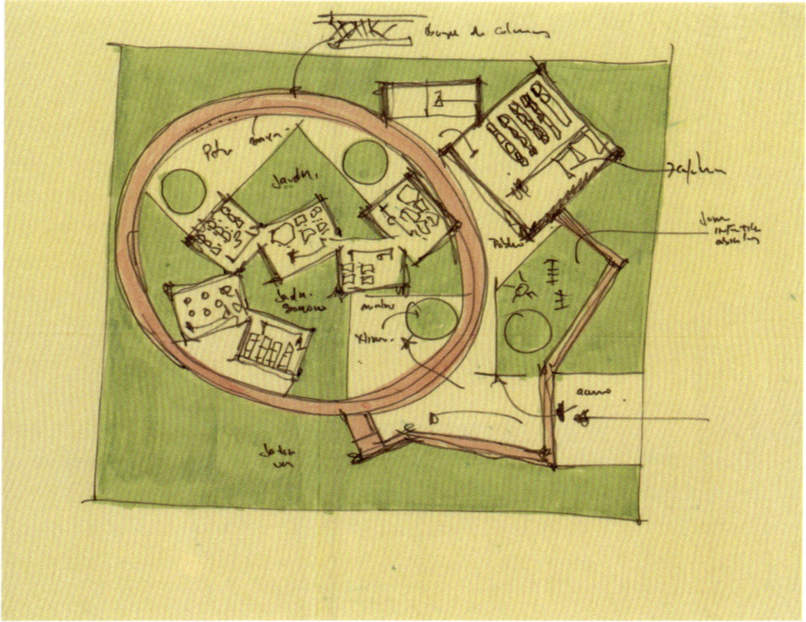

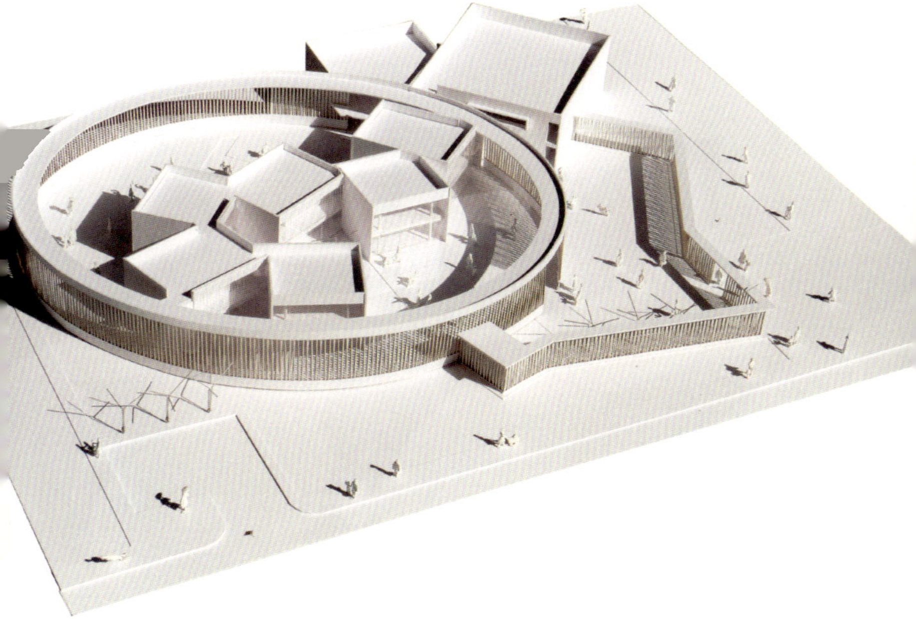

Modules, pieces, bands

Modular systems are open and flexible, made up of individual elements that can be composed and adapted to different external conditions. In architecture, they give rise to projects predisposed to grow, change and be shaped in keeping with topographical, programmatic and urban parameters, particular circumstances or developments that occur over time. These are strategies devised more in terms of method than an established formal result: they exist only by virtue of their capacity for transformation. The architecture that arises from this approach thus rests on versatile systems, unfinished, and they evolve as molecular aggregates. Once again, play can be instrument for controlling them: by adding piece after piece, the system can grow even outside the architect's control.

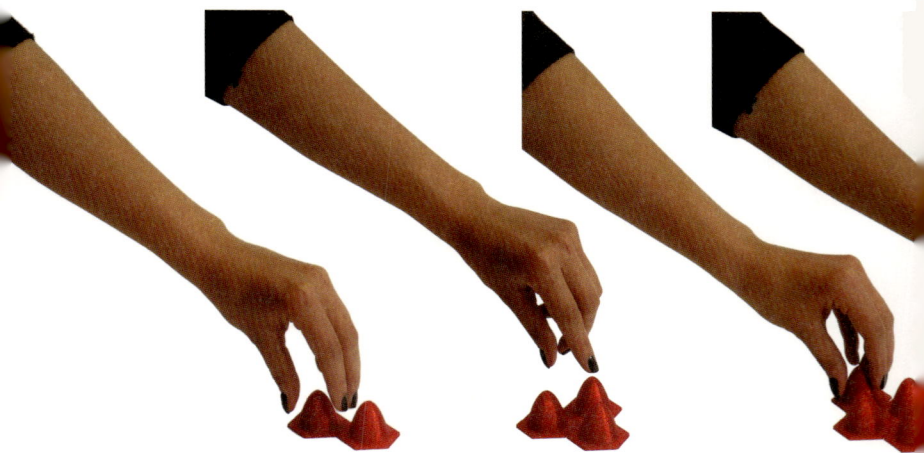

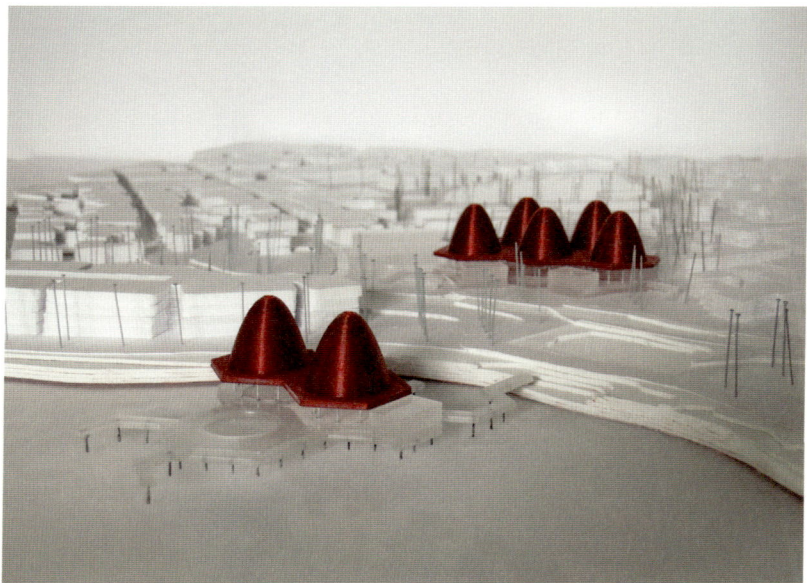

**Barrios ConSentidos public space
and community center**
Argos Foundation
Cartagena, Colombia, 2014
Toys and model

**Barrios ConSentidos public space
and community center**
Argos Foundation
Cartagena, Colombia, 2014
Plan studies and modular systems

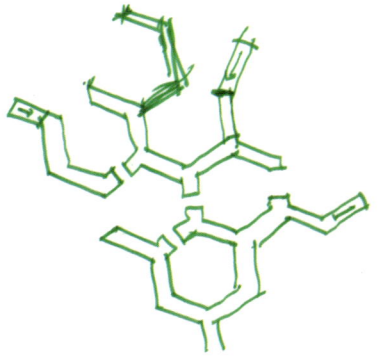

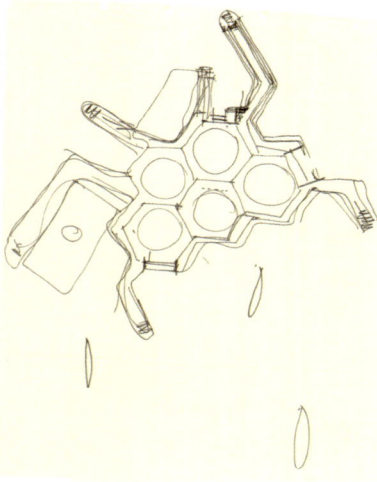

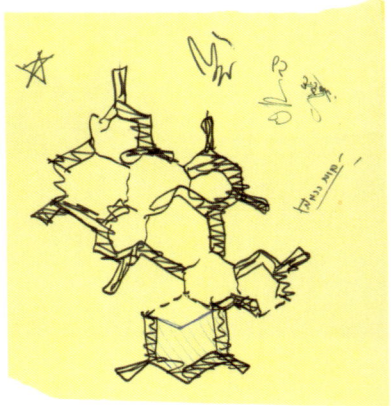

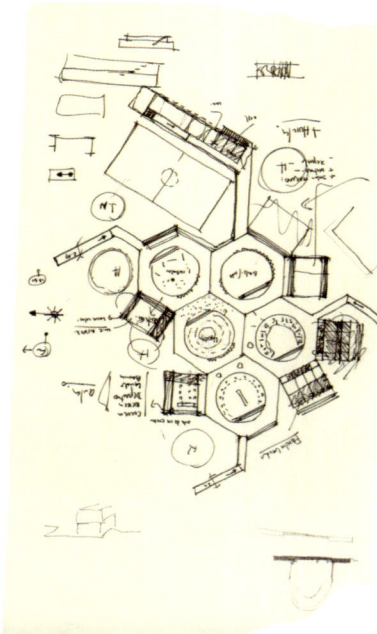

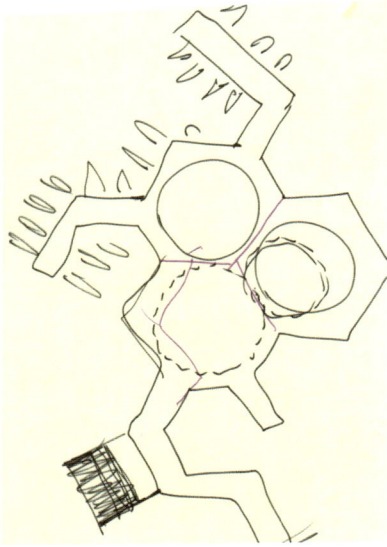

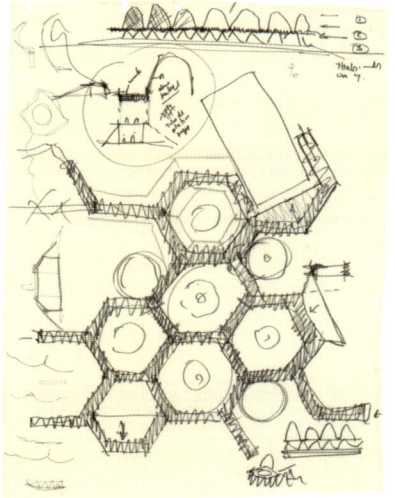

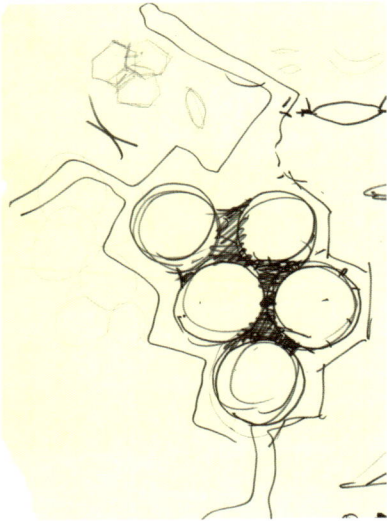

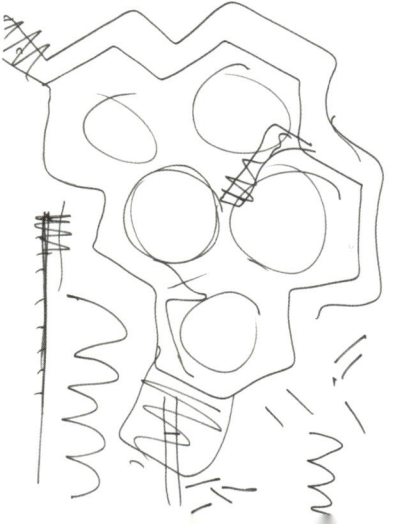

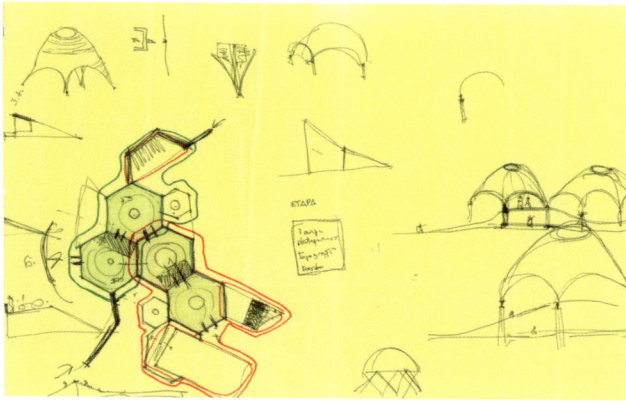

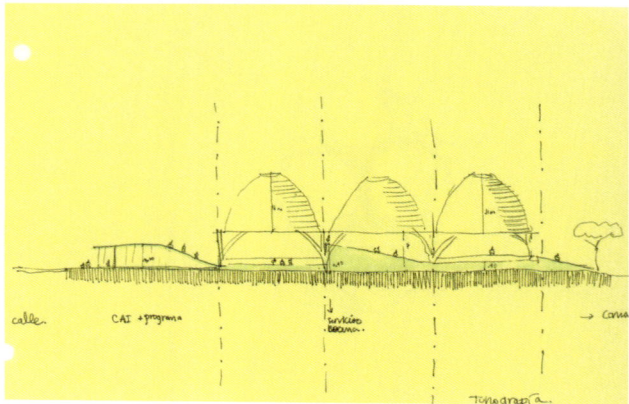

**Barrios ConSentidos
public space and
community center**
Argos Foundation
Cartagena, Colombia,
2014
Sketches, drawings
and models

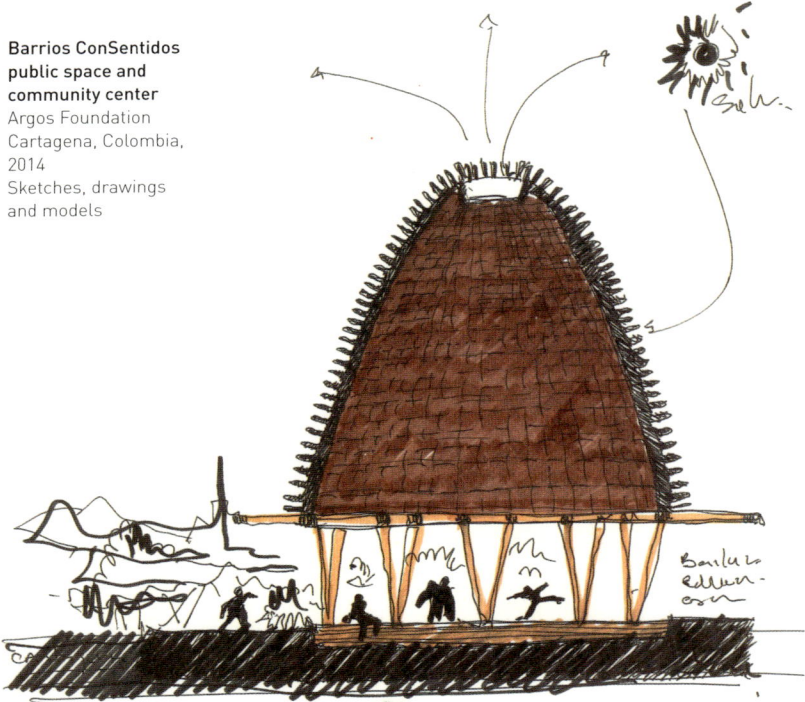

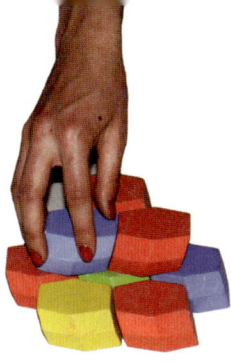

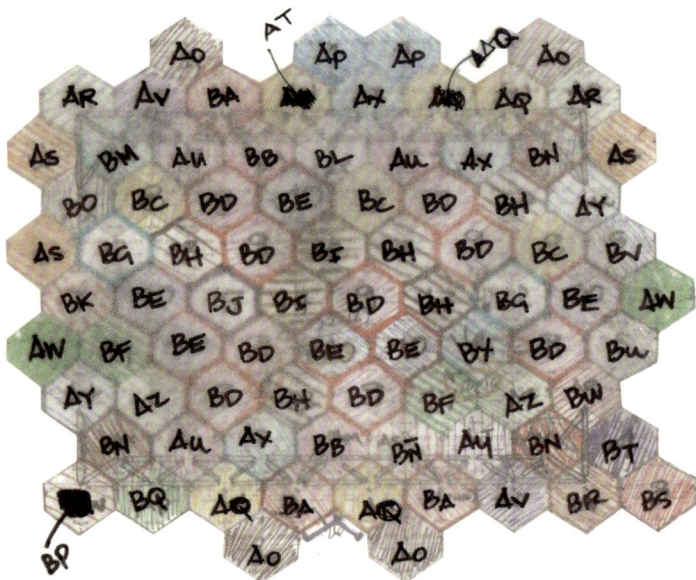

CIELO RASO
NIVEL 02

Forest of hope
Pies Descalzos Foundation
Cazucá, Colombia, 2011
Toys and diagrams: molecular aggregates
and architectural diagrams

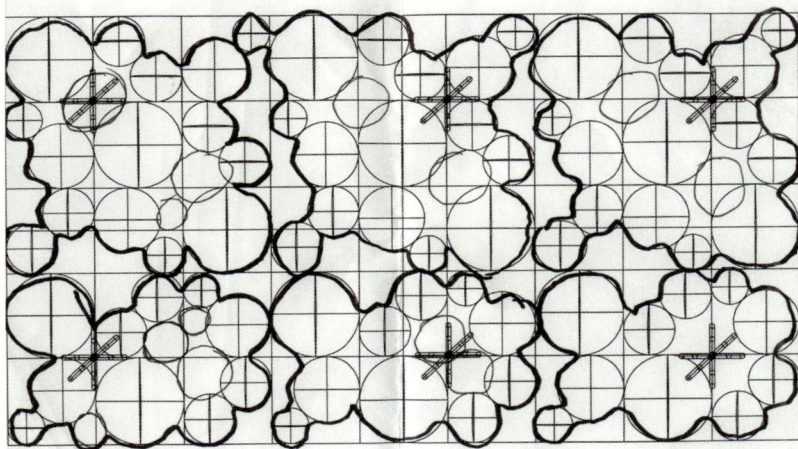

CALUCA → Sistema de Crecimento modular.

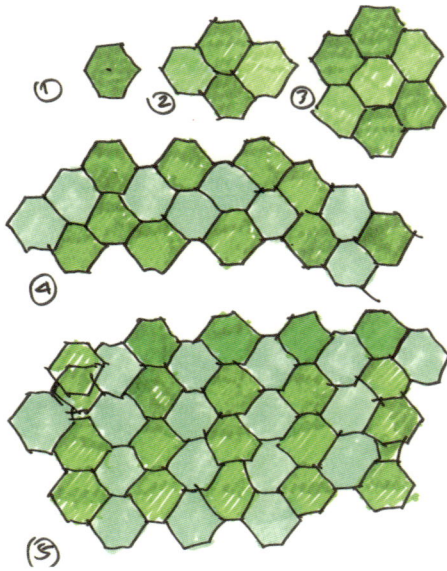

① ② ③

④

⑤

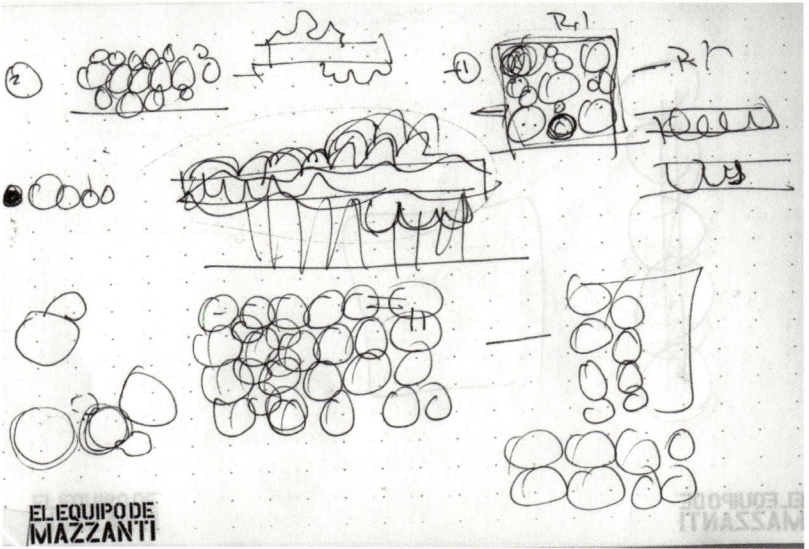

these and previous pages
Forest of hope Pies Descalzos Foundation
Cazucá, Colombia, 2011
Study sketches and models: molecular
aggregates and architectural form

Coliseos
Four Sport Scenarios
for the 2010 South
American Games
with Felipe Mesa
(Plan B Arquitectos)
Medellin, Colombia,
2009
Sketches and digital
models

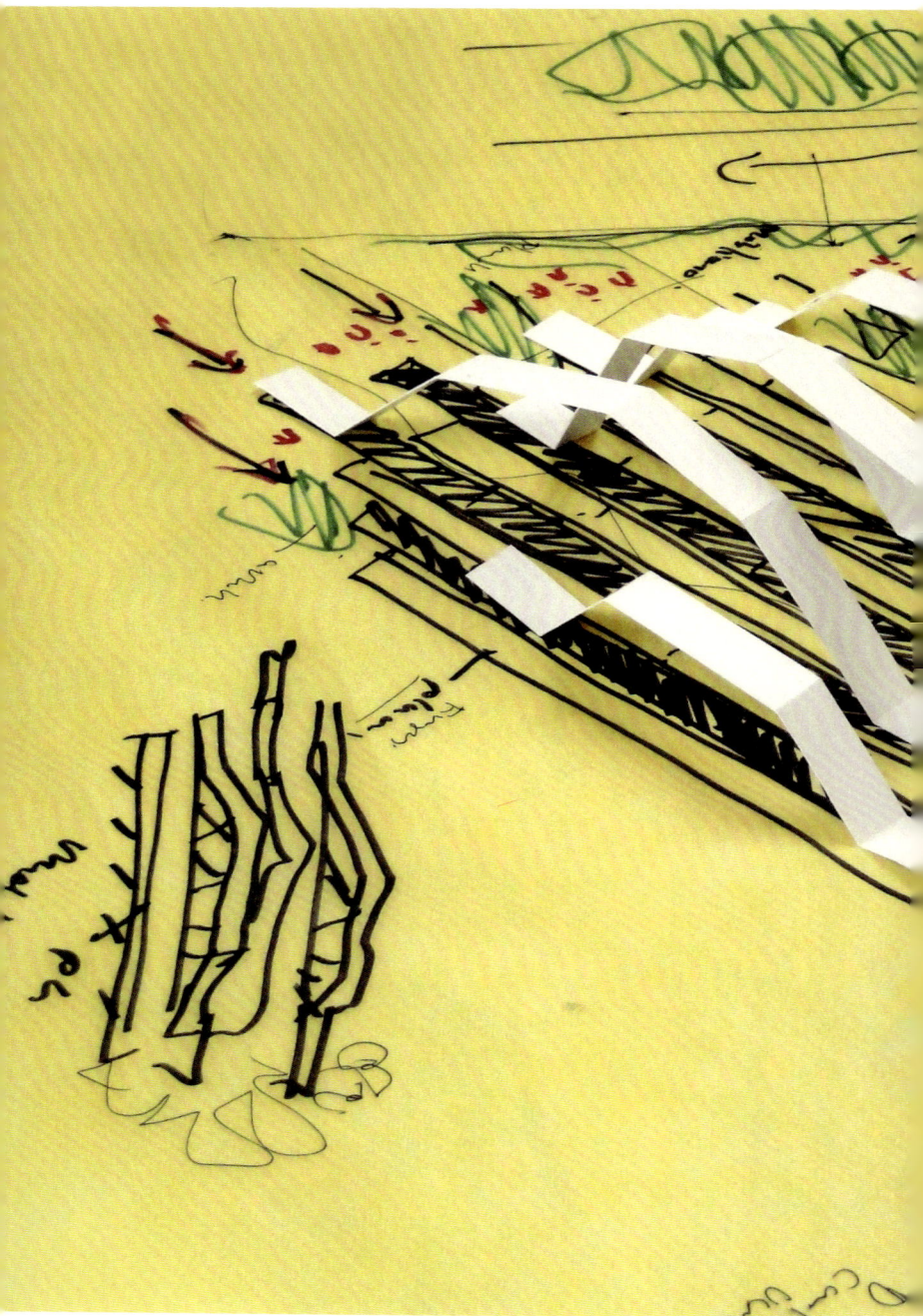

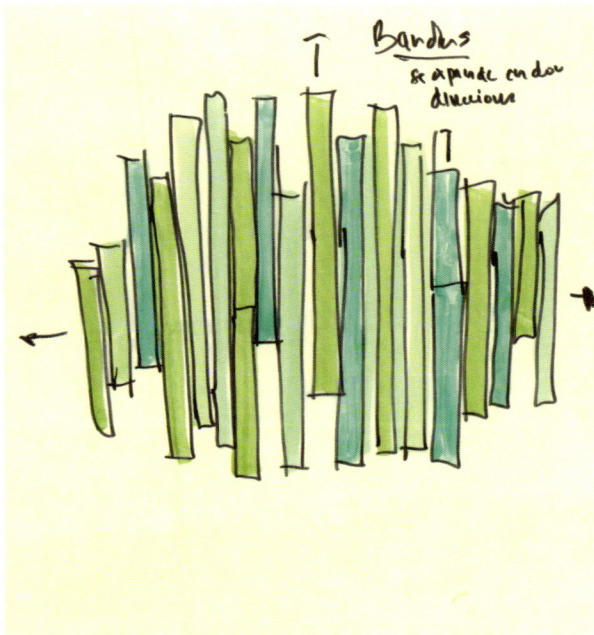

Bandas
se apunde en dou direcciou

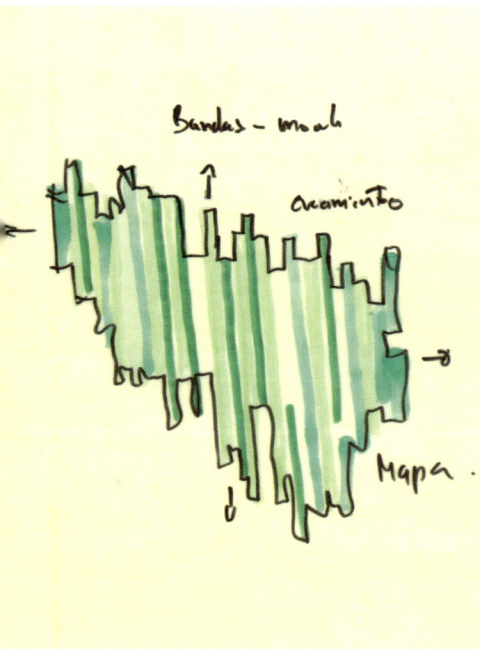

Bandas – mah

acamiento

Mapa.

Adapkis

achu

avu

78

Coliseos
Four Sport Scenarios for the 2010
South American Games
with Felipe Mesa (Plan B Arquitectos)
Medellin, Colombia, 2009
previous pages Paper model with sketch
these pages Bands and growth systems

sistema de bandas
de crecimiento en dos sentidos
un estrategia + que un DIseño

medellin en montañas.
geografia

geografia

Coliseos
Four Sport Scenarios
for the 2010 South
American Games
with Felipe Mesa
(Plan B Arquitectos)
Medellin, Colombia,
2009
Bands and growth
systems: sketches
and toys

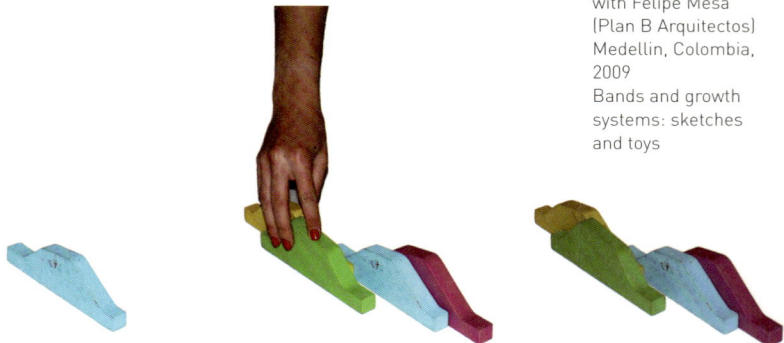

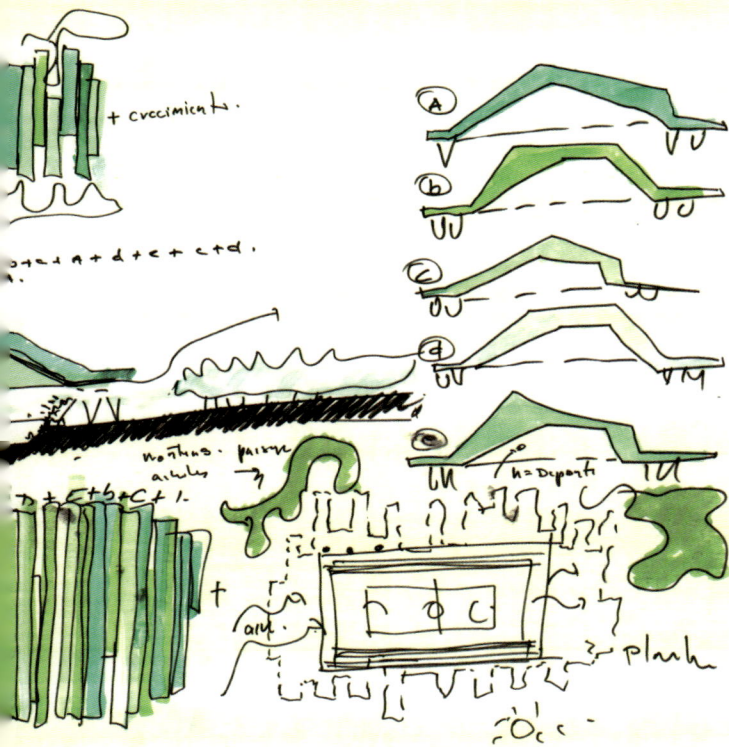

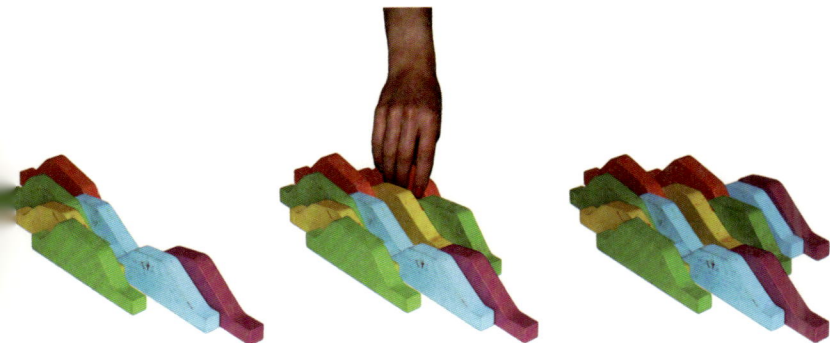

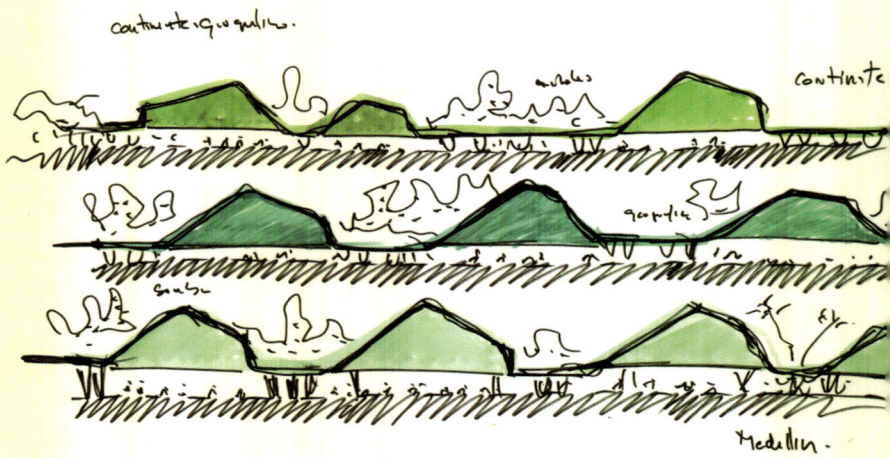

Coliseos
Four Sport Scenarios for the 2010
South American Games with Felipe Mesa
(Plan B Arquitectos)
Medellin, Colombia, 2009
From landscape to building. Section studies

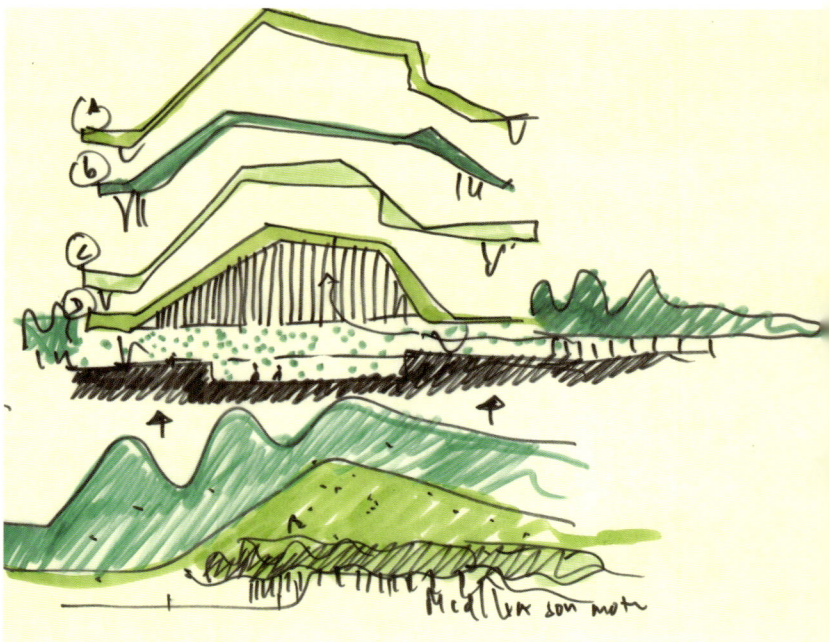

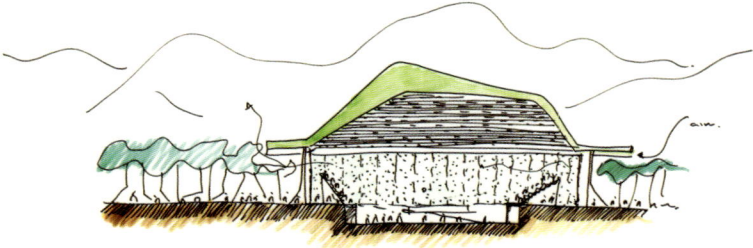

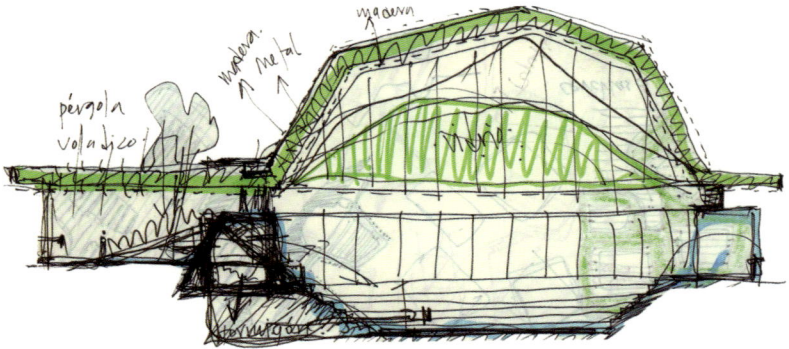

pérgola
voladizo

clima

Pies Descalzos School
Pies Descalzos Foundation
Cartagena, Colombia, 2014
these pages Sketches and toys
following pages Aggregation models

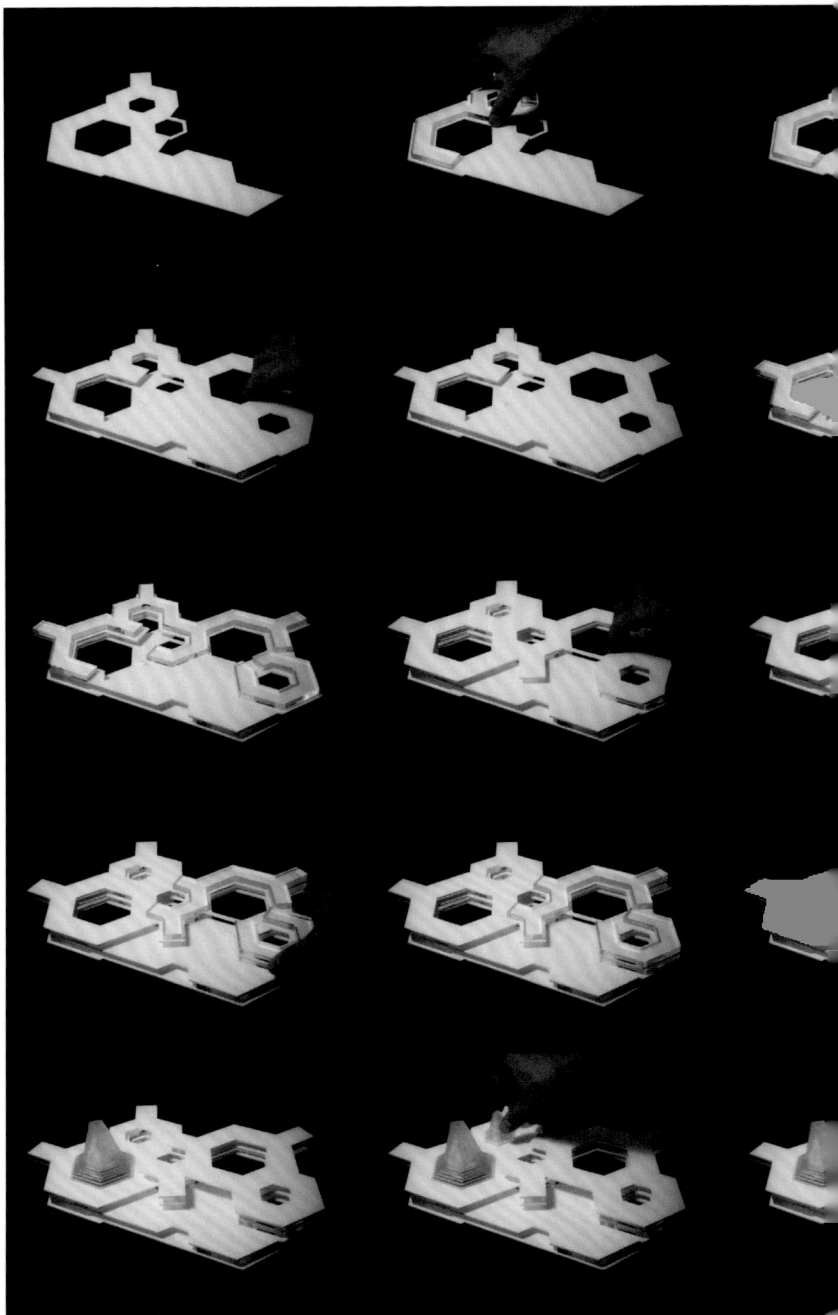

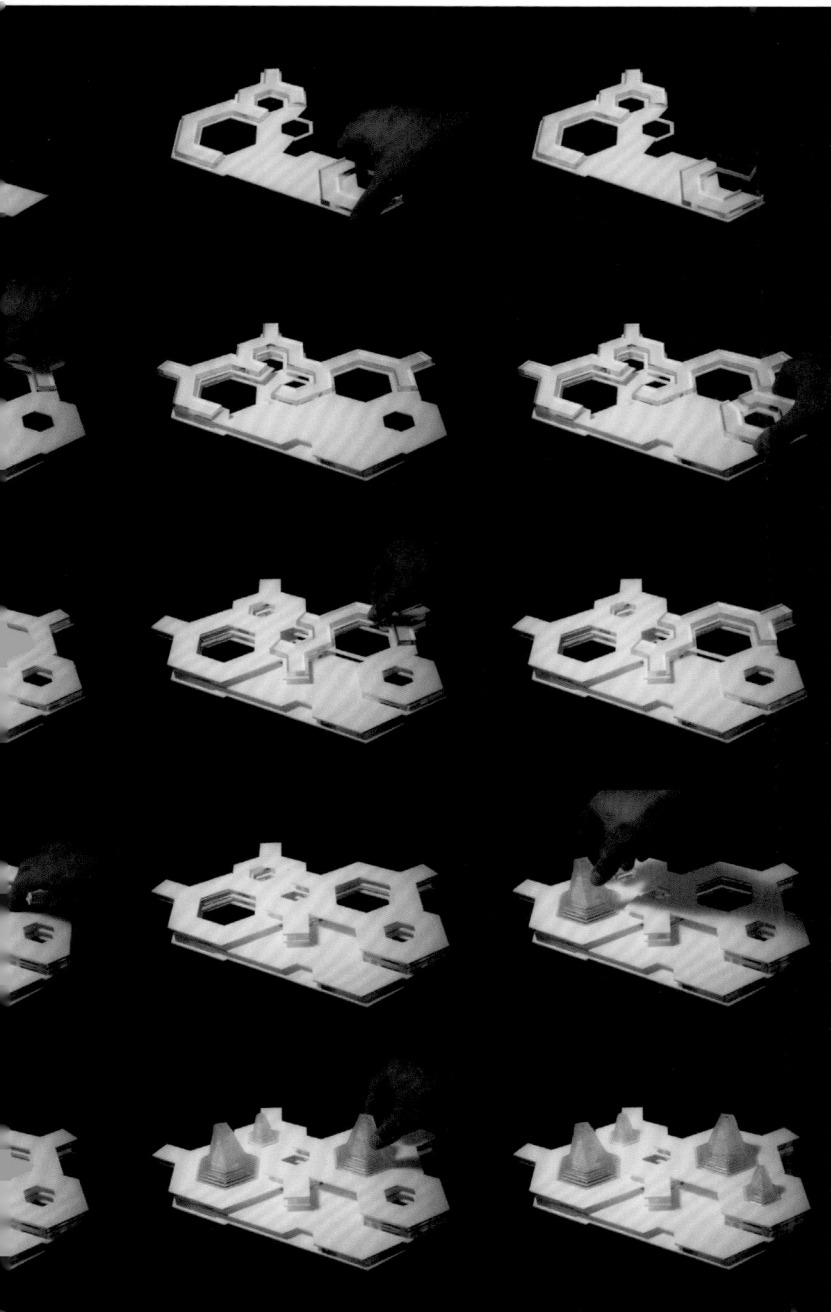

Pies Descalzos School
Pies Descalzos Foundation
Cartagena, Colombia, 2014
Models and sketches

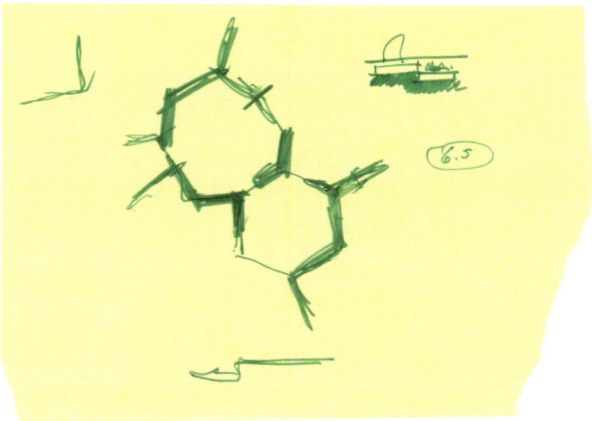

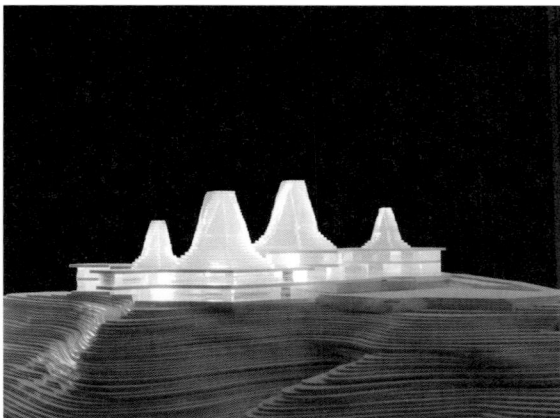

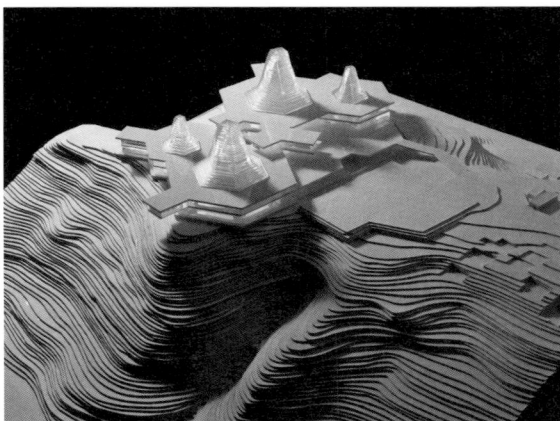

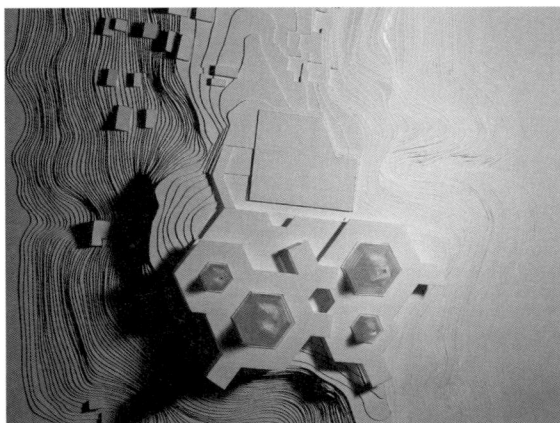

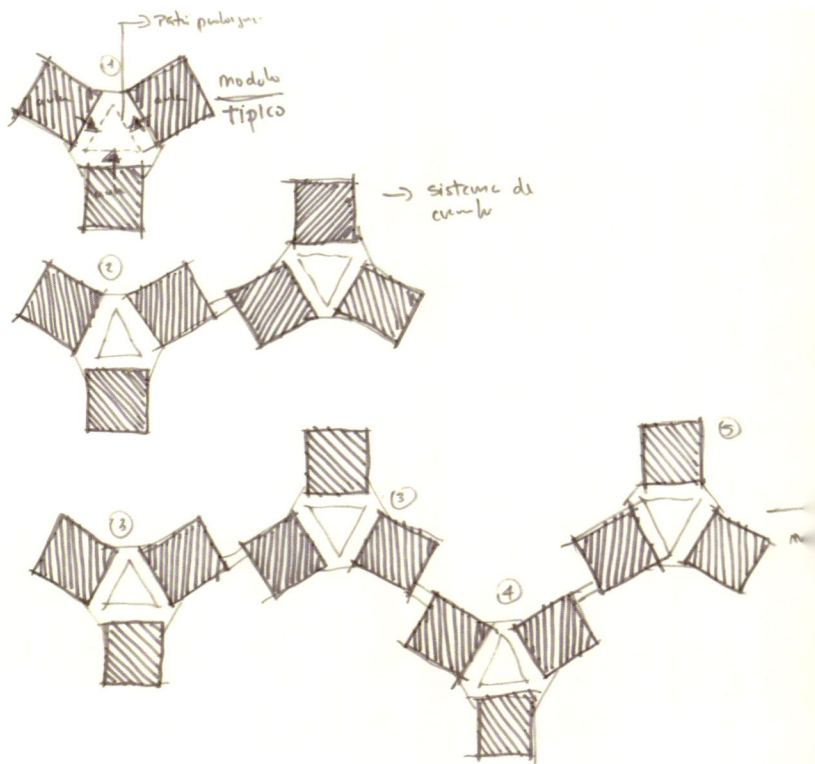

→ Peti perbargas

① modulo tipico

→ sistema de cuemba

②

③

④

⑤

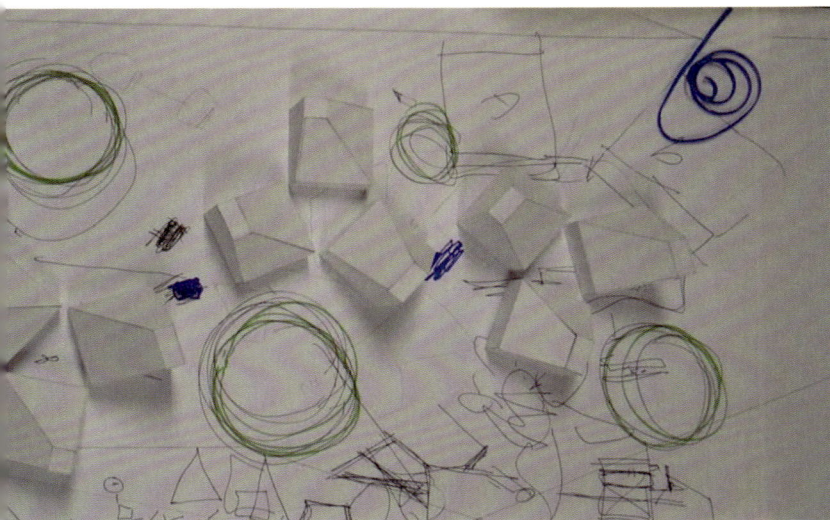

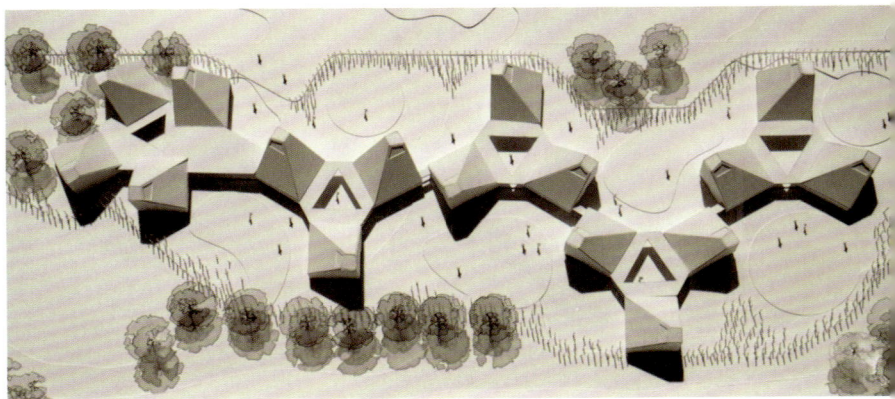

these and following pages
Timayui Kindergarten
Carulla foundation AEIOTU
Santa Marta, Colombia, 2011
Growth systems. Toys, models and sketches

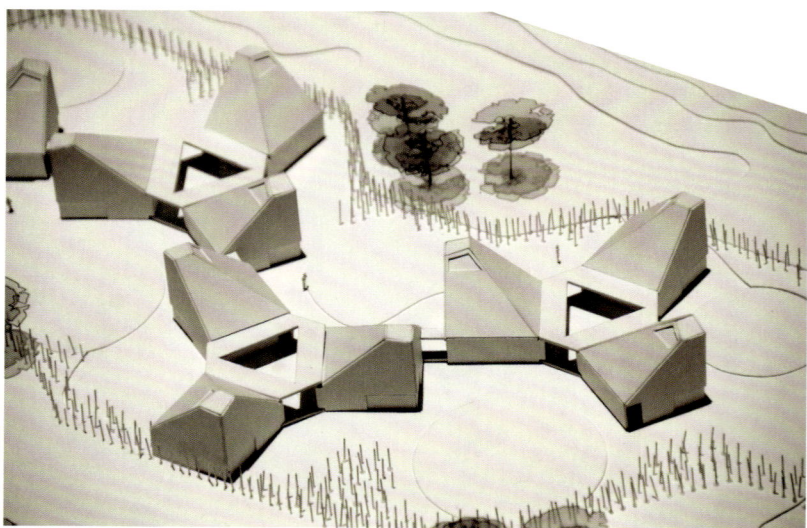

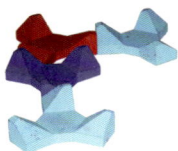

tnnqvi

Flom

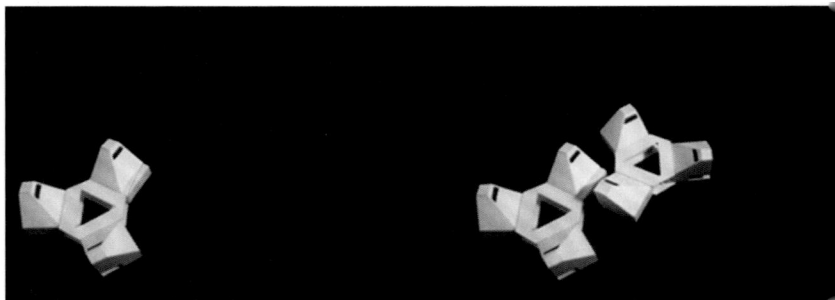

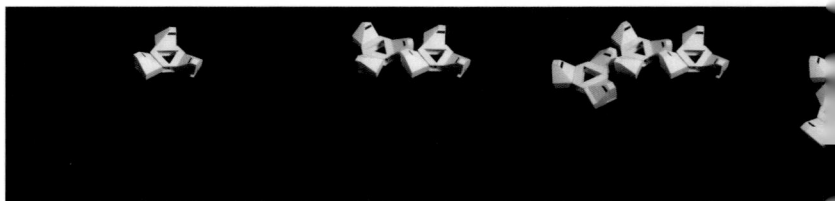

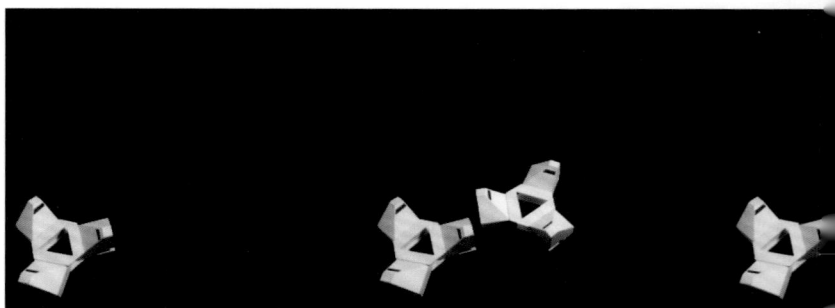

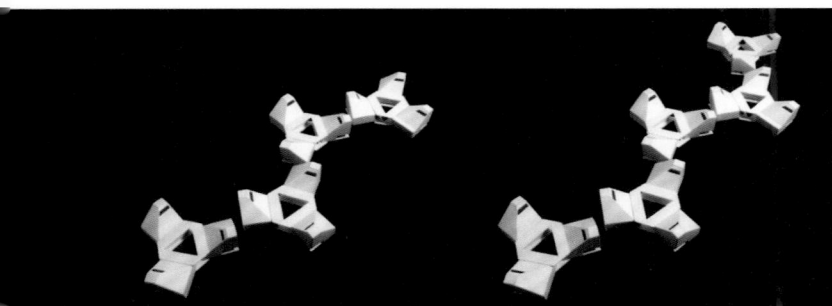

Timayui Kindergarten
Carulla foundation AEIOTU
Santa Marta, Colombia, 2011
Evolut on studies

Roots and growth models

Models of growth, ramifications and textures function as abstract systems of organization, making it possible to develop open-ended strategies. These systems enable spatial flexibility, resting on repetitive elements and an orderly expansion. Direction and dimension become key factors to ensure functionality in the projects. They are elastic codes, without scale or limits, in which order is rooted in the principles guiding their evolution.

El Equipo Mazzanti seeks unfinished configurations based on tree structures capable of generating open forms: systems that can expand and connect through new branches that follow changes and specific conditions. This mode of operation makes it possible to link different points by establishing relations between urban, social, spatial and environmental conditions.

San Cristóbal Library Park Competition
with Felipe Mesa (Plan B Arquitectos)
Medellin, Colombia, 2009
Toys

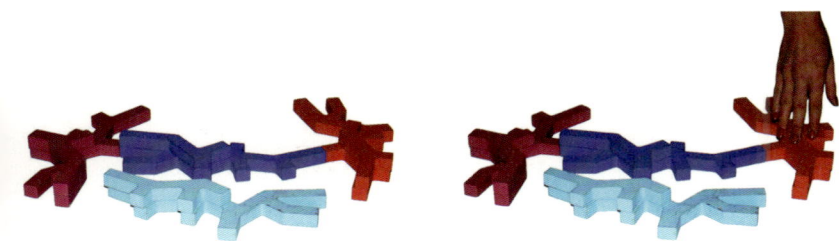

San Cristóbal Library Park Competition
with Felipe Mesa (Plan B Arquitectos)
Medellin, Colombia, 2009
Models

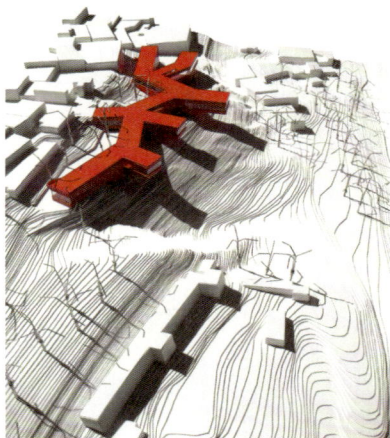

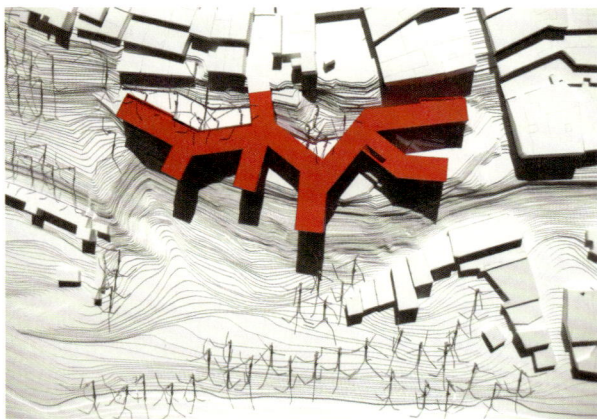

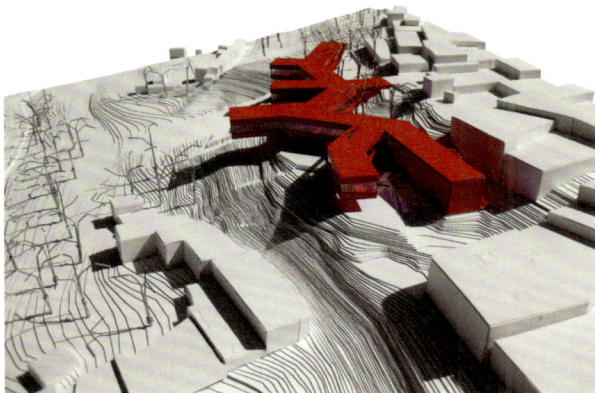

**Javeriana
University
Science Faculty
Competition**
Bogotà, Colombia,
2016
Sketches

Marinilla Educational Park
Marinilla, Colombia, 2015
Sketch

Marinilla Educational Park
Marinilla, Colombia, 2015
Toys and sketches

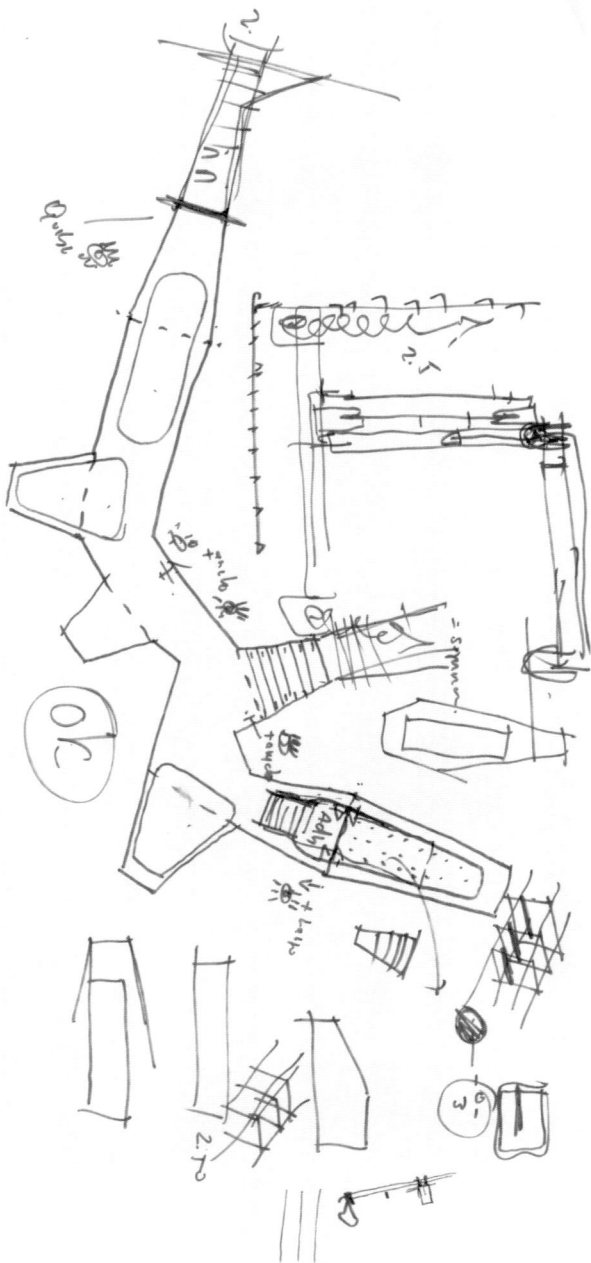

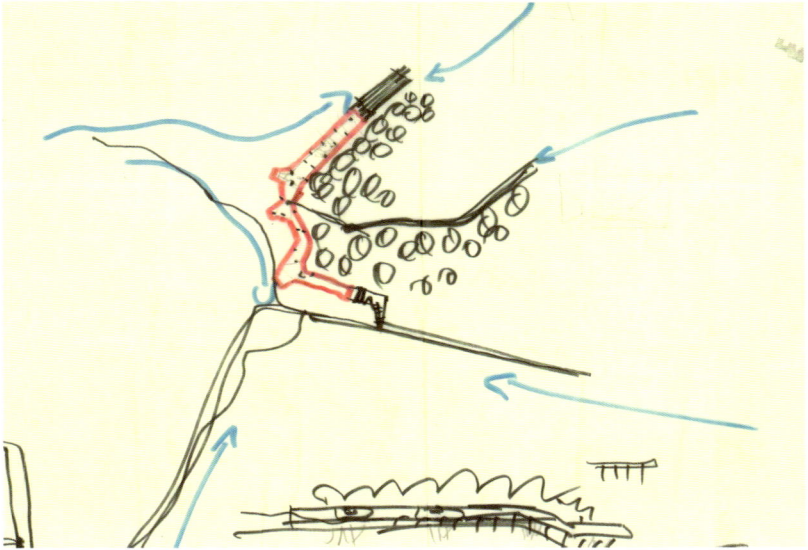

Marinilla Educational Park
Marinilla, Colombia, 2015
Plan studies and model

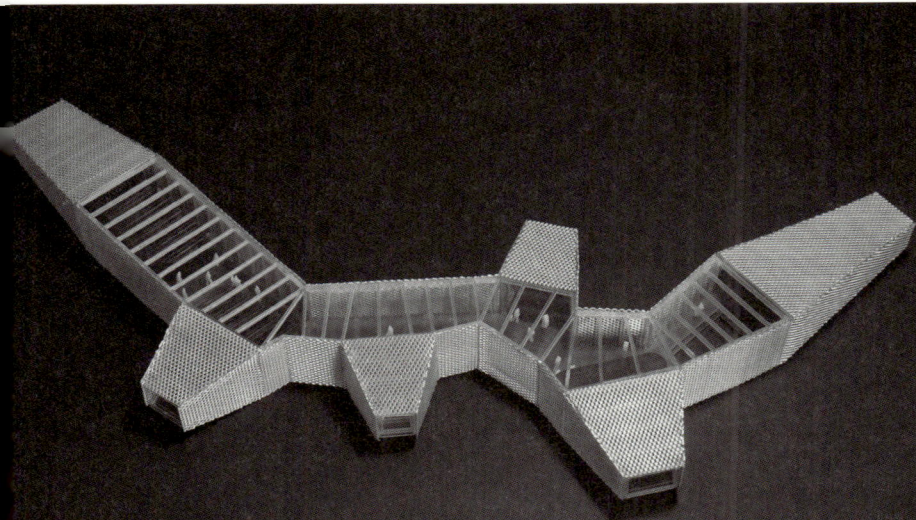

these and following pages
Marinilla Educational Park
Marinilla, Colombia, 2015
Plan studies

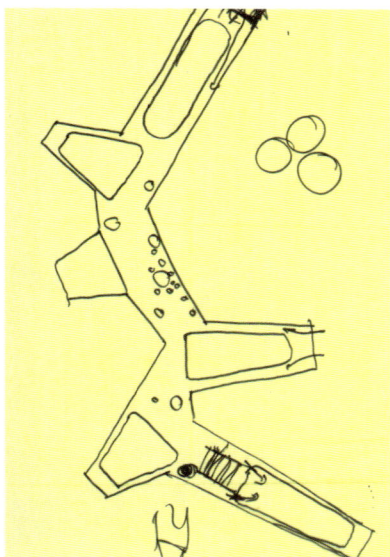

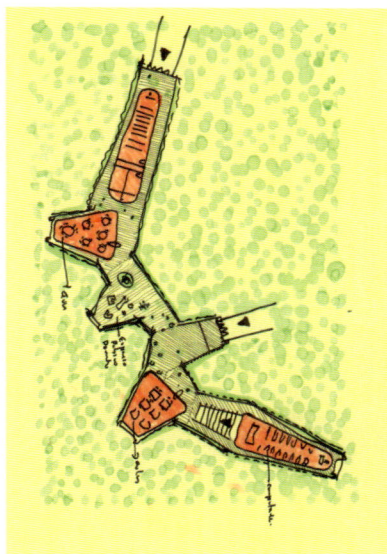

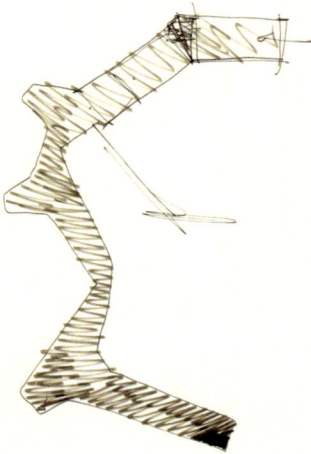

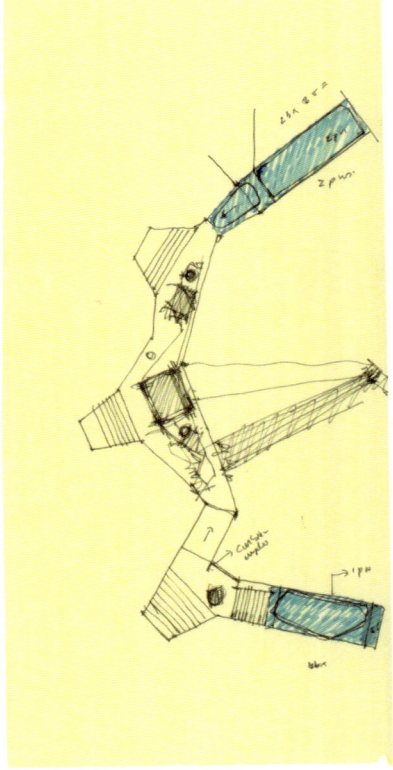

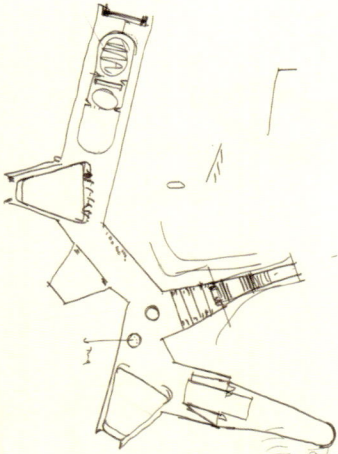

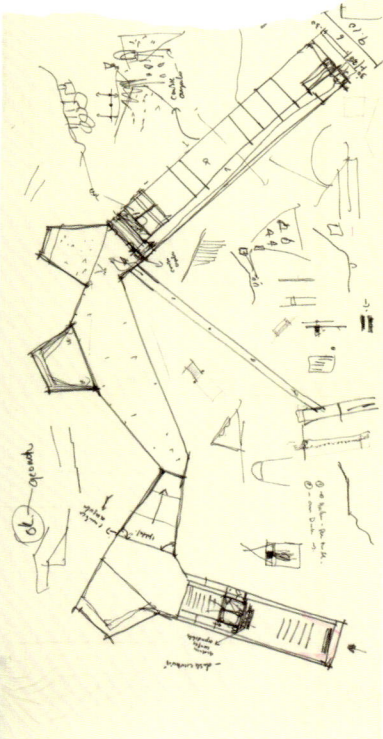

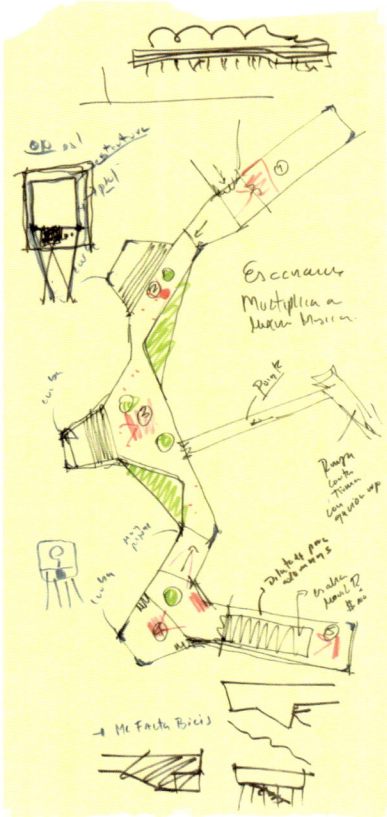

Colombian football team housing competition
Bogotá, Colombia, 2009
these pages Toys and study models
following pages Sketches

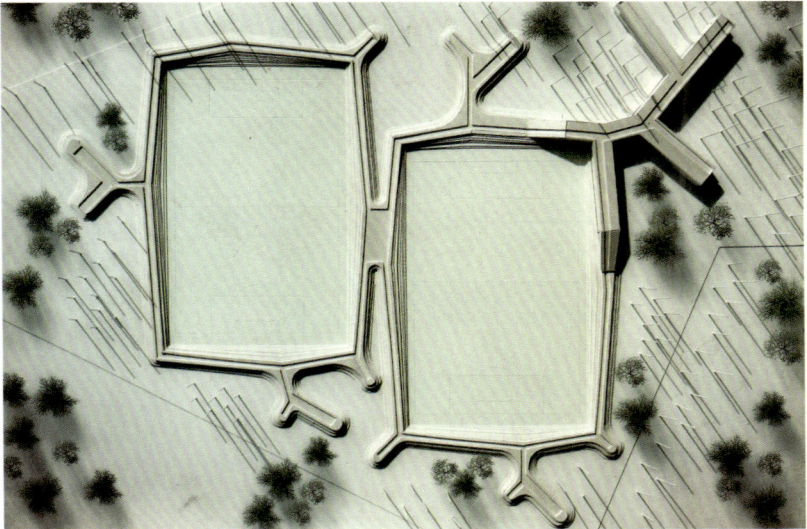

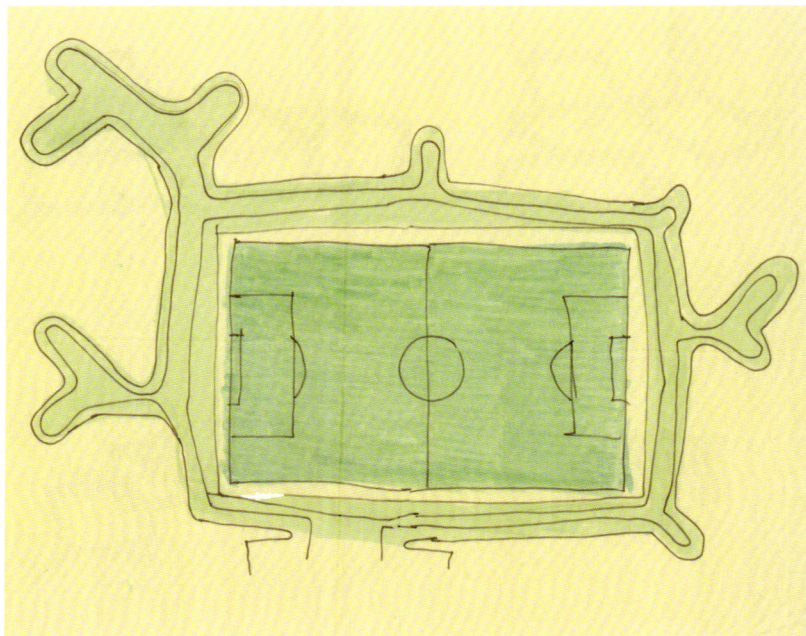

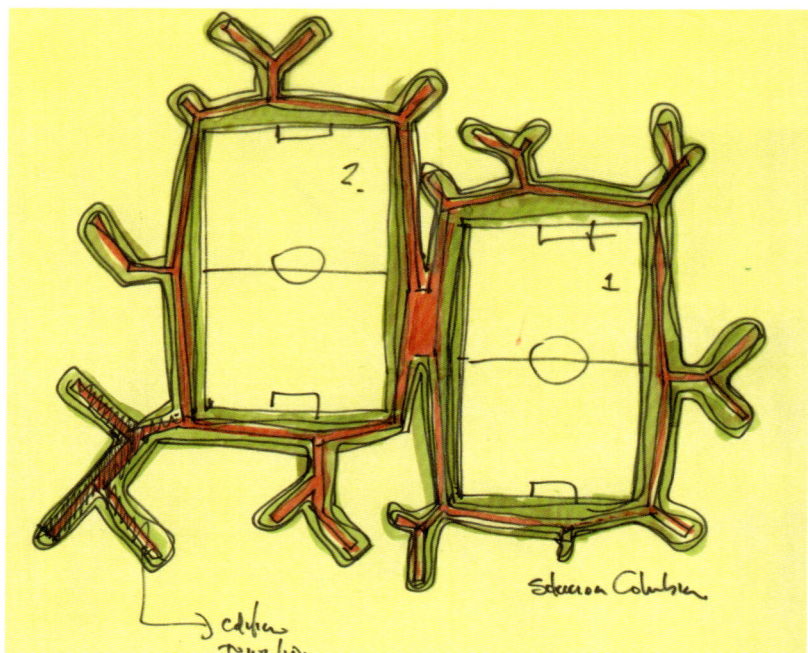

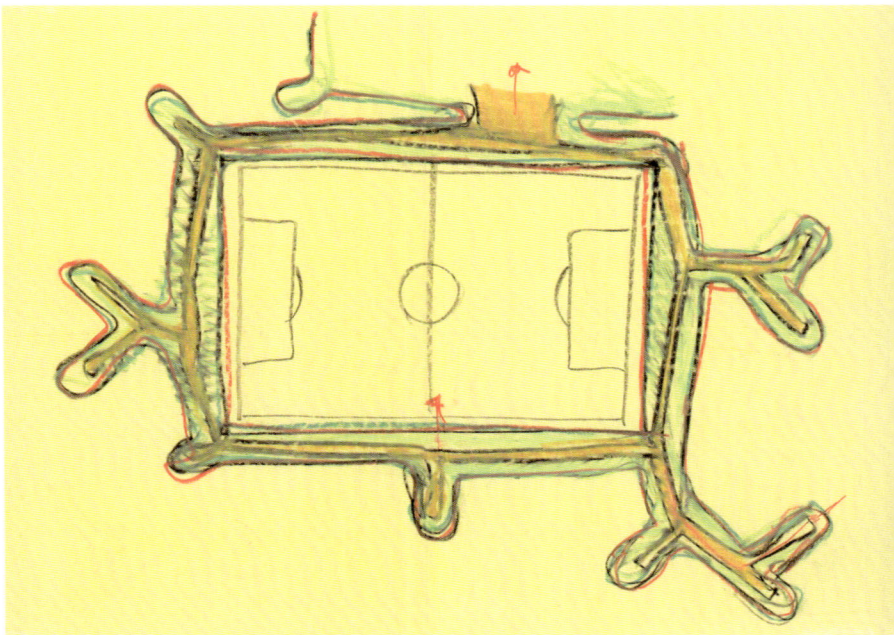

Sólmeo Holl

Selección Colombia.

Landscapes, topographies and geographies

El Equipo Mazzanti aims to develop not so much architectural objects as landscapes, geographies and urban
topographies, establishing a tacit pact with the natural
world. The relation between the project and its context
is extended to become, once more, an operative mechanism: starting from ripples, folds and incisions, the relations between landscape and architecture are recast,
fading and dissolving the ties between figure and ground.
This approach merges organic and technological, the
natural and the urban environment, so creating hybrid
forms that explore the role of nature in contemporary
life. The project takes root in its context, merges with its
setting and creates new textures that deform and transform the existing, making it recognizable. So, in a city like
Medellin, where the topography is marked by mountains,
the architecture becomes part of those mountains by
conceiving unusual geographies.

Spain Library Park - Santo Domingo Savio
Medellin, Colombia, 2005
right Medellin with mountains
below diagrams for the library

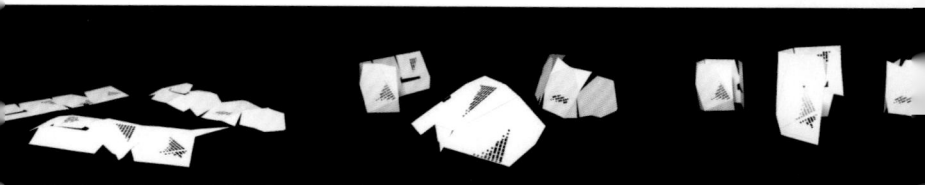

Medelln con montañas. -

Spain Library Park - Santo Domingo Savio
Medellin, Colombia, 2005
The library and its contest:
study sketches

Medellín son montañas y
geografías.

Montañas

Valle. — Aburra.

La biblioteca son
montañas y geografía.

Nacen de la
montaña

y son montaña

son parte de la
geografía

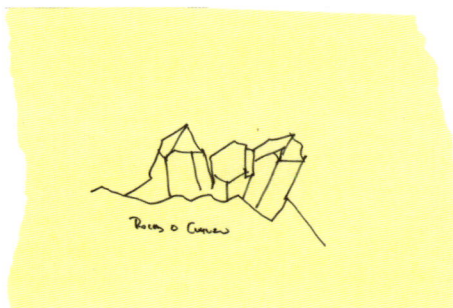

Spain Library Park - Santo Domingo Savio
Medellin, Colombia, 2005
Study models and sketch

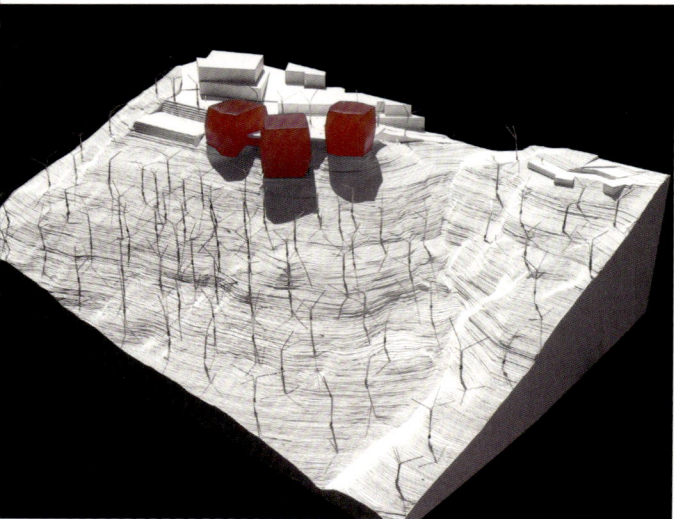

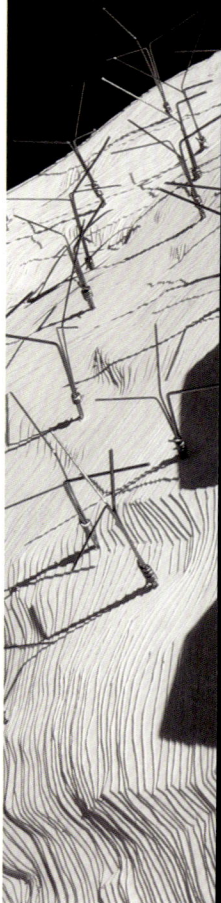

monkentas.

Nivel calla

La arqitectura/ en Barranbon en comi.

Un edificio que se fud con en monluti.

Bogotá's Spain Cultural Center Competition
with Felipe Mesa (Plan B Arquitectos)
Bogotá, Colombia, 2007
Elevation studies

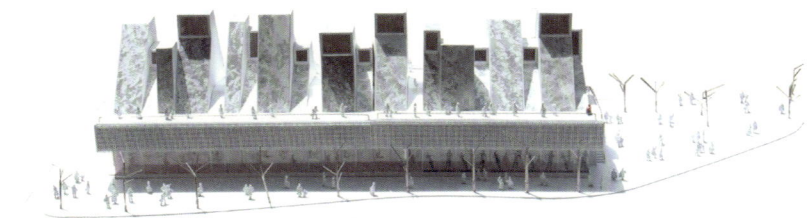

Bogotá's Spain Cultural Center Competition
with Felipe Mesa (Plan B Arquitectos)
Bogotá, Colombia, 2007
Toys

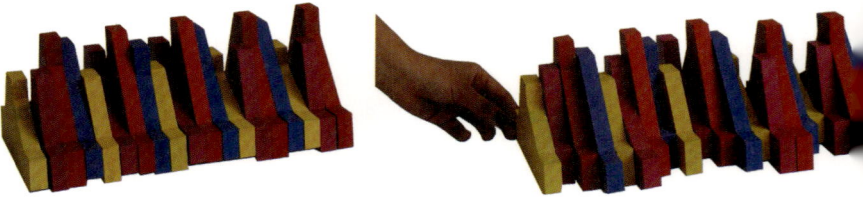

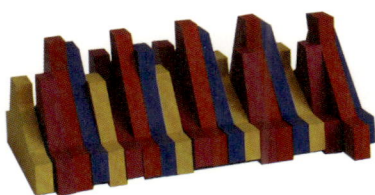

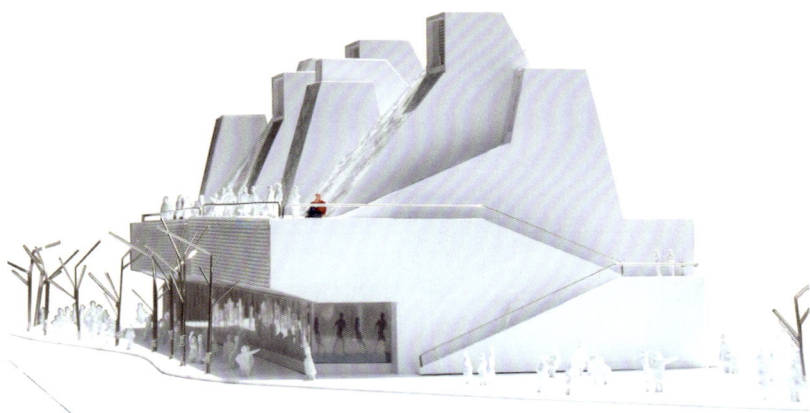

Bogotá's Spain Cultural Center Competition
with Felipe Mesa (Plan B Arquitectos)
Bogotá, Colombia, 2007
Models

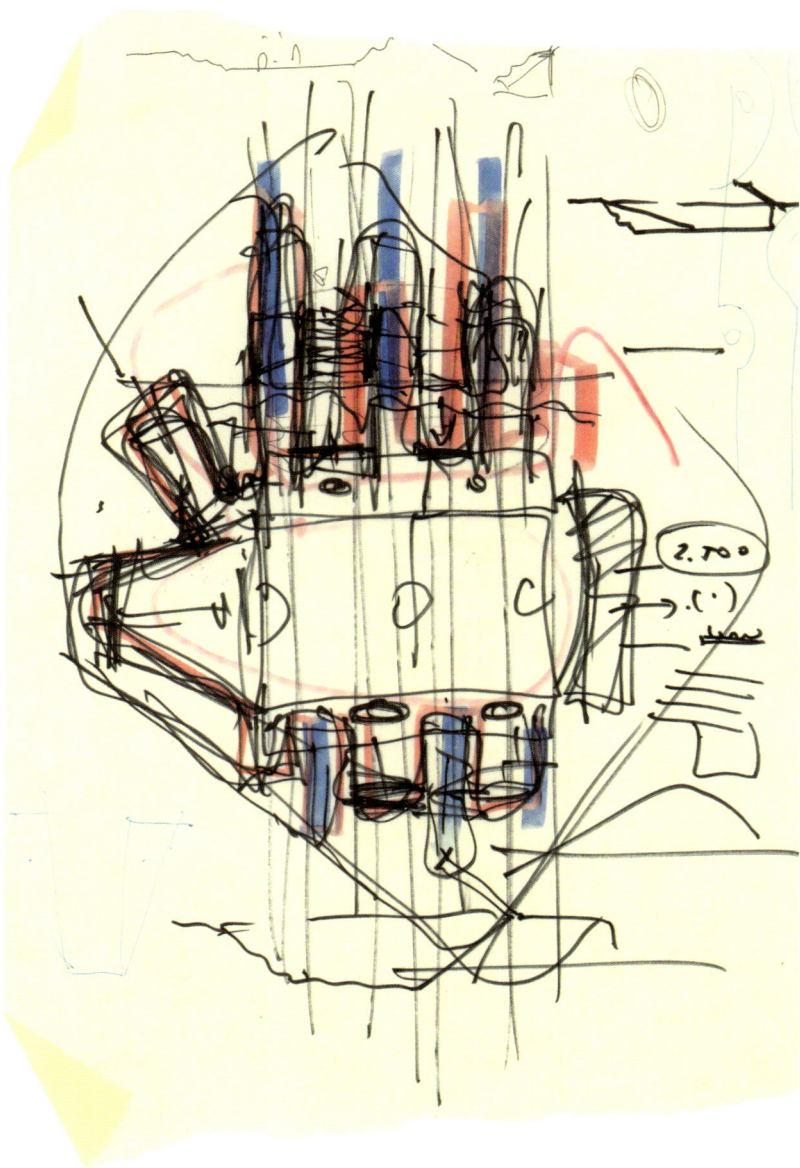

these and following pages
Romelio Martinez Soccer Stadium
Barranquilla, Colombia, 2015
Sketches and models

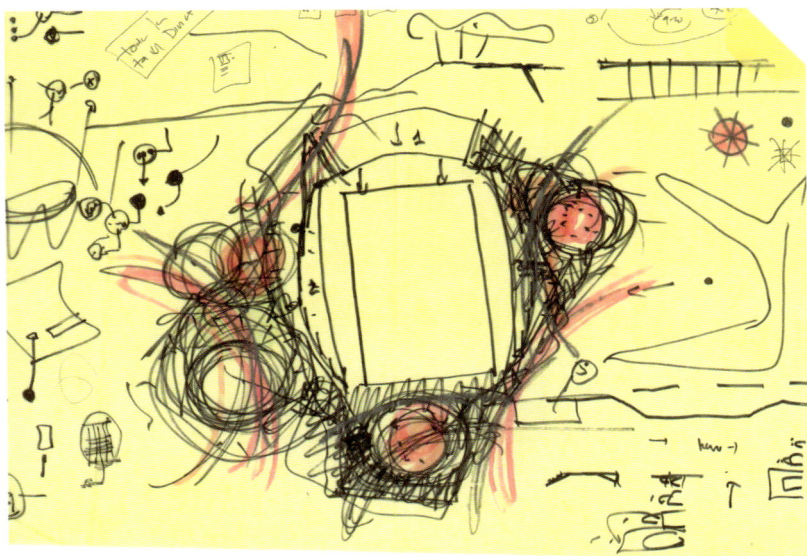

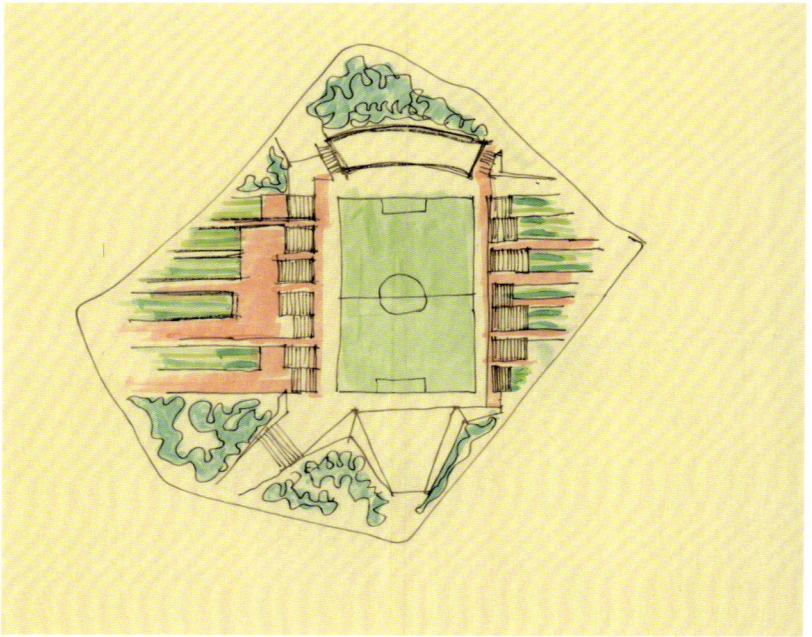

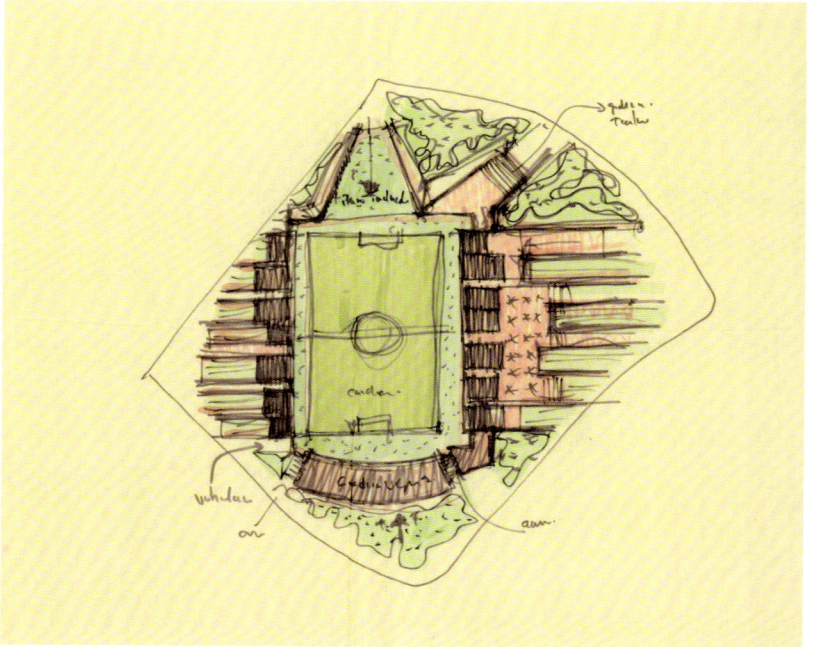

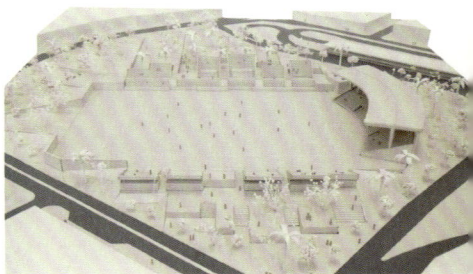
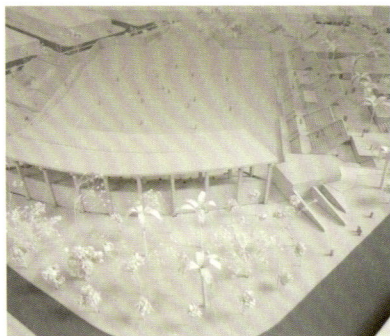
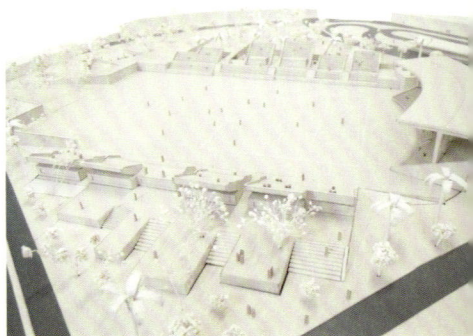

Capillas de la Fé Cemetery
La Calera, Colombia, 2016
Model

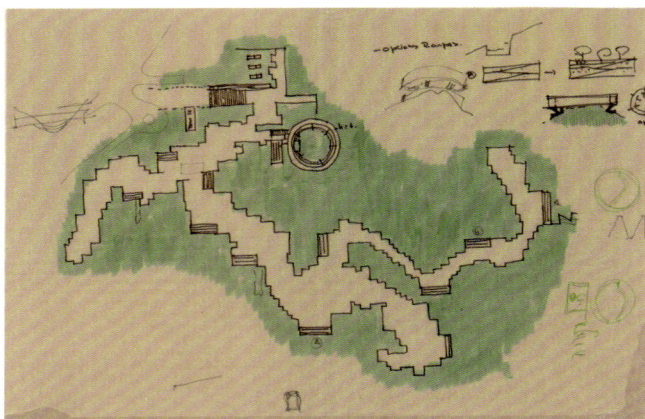

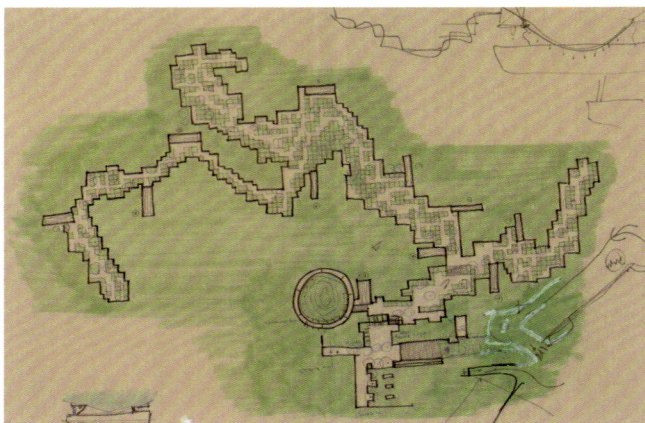

these pages
Capillas de la Fé Cemetery
La Calera, Colombia, 2016
Study sketches and model

following pages
Paramaribo river master plan
with Geografia Urbana
Paramaribo, Suriname, 2016
Study sketches

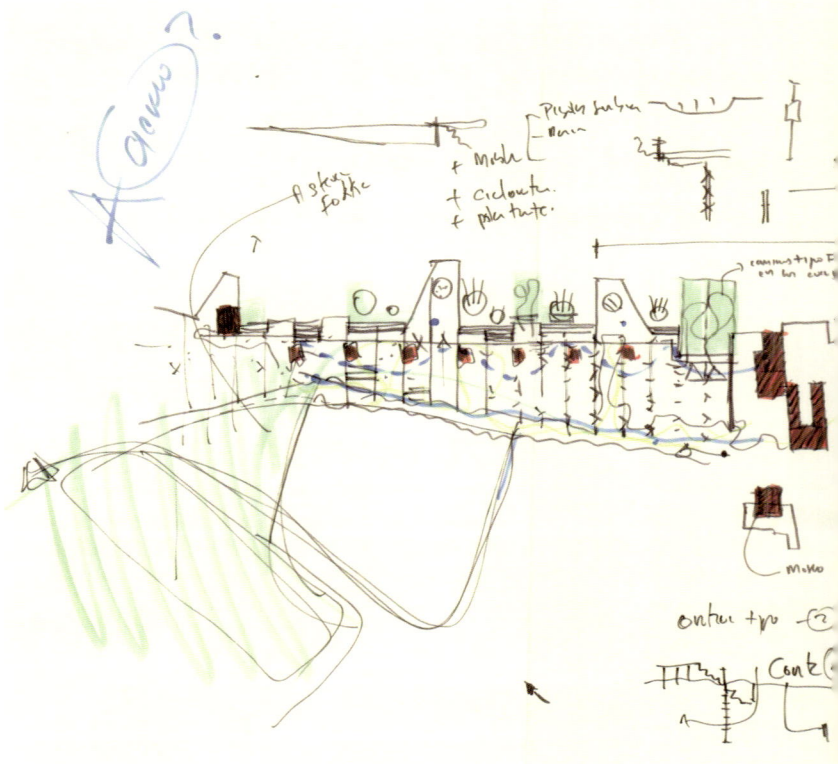

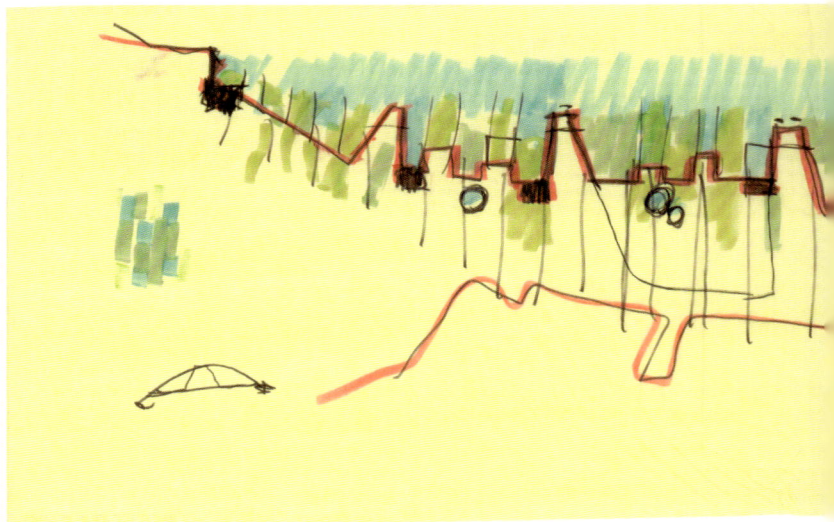

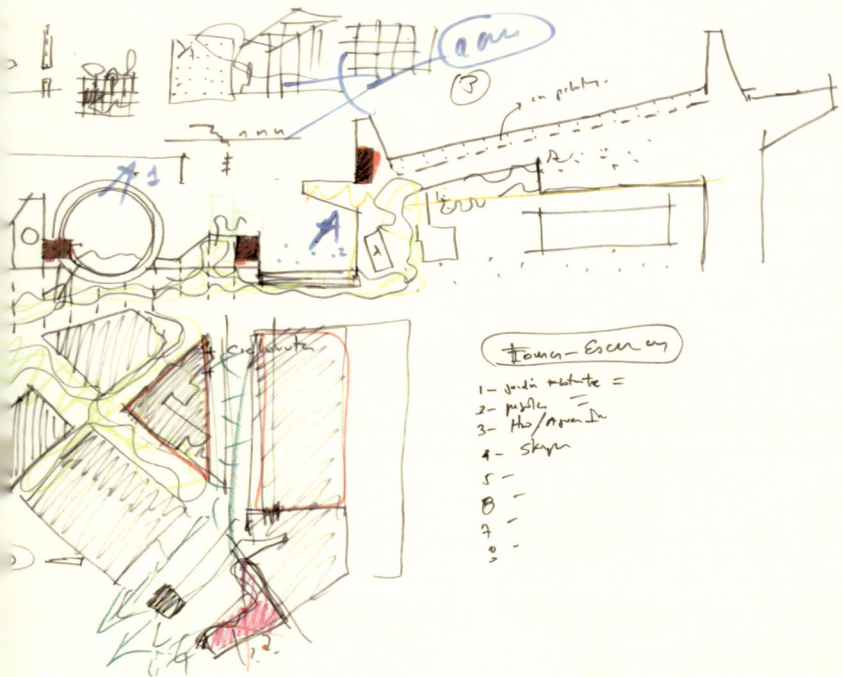

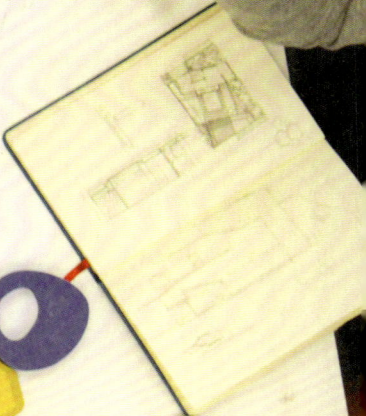

Biography

Giancarlo Mazzanti (Barranquilla, Colombia – 1963) studied architecture at the Universidad Javeriana in Bogotá (1987), and then specialized in History and Theory of Architecture and Industrial Design at the University of Florence, Italy (1991). He has been full professor at various universities, including the Universidad de los Andes, Princeton, Upen, Columbia and Harvard. His work has been published in over 500 national and international reviews, and he has taken part in 15 exhibitions and delivered 70 lectures worldwide, at universities and elsewhere.

During twenty-nine years of professional experience, his work has been distinguished for its collaborative and team-based approach. Hence his adoption of the name El Equipo Mazzanti: his projects involve over 57 design groups, biologists, planners, artists and philosophers, and many others.

Equipo Mazzanti's work is characterized by a marked social commitment and an innovative and critical approach to projects. The basic premise is that the value of architecture is rooted not just in itself, but in what it produces in social and behavioral terms.

Mazzanti is notable as a winner of two Bienales Colombianas de Arquitectura; he also won the Bienal Iberoamericana in the category of best architectural work (2008, Lisbon, Portugal), the Bienal Panamericana de Arquitectura in the architectural design category (2008), the Colombian Lápiz de Acero y Lápiz de Acero Azul, the Global award for Sustainable Achitecture (2010, Paris, France), and has been recognized by FastCompany magazine as representing one of the world's ten most innovative architectural practices. Last February 2017, Giancarlo was named Honorary Fellow by The American Institute of Architects.

His work has been selected by the MoMA in New York, the Centre Georges Pompidou in Paris and the Carnegie Museum of Art in Pittsburg to become part of their permanent collections with designs and models. In 2016 his design for the Parque Educativo de Marinilla won the gold medal at the American Architecture Prize and the Next Landmark award (Berlin).

El Equipo Mazzanti has its headquarters in Bogotá with a branch office in Madrid, and is notable for the development of projects in the most diverse contexts in America and Europe, having developed more than a hundred public and private buildings that have become outstanding examples of community construction.

Credits

Francesca Serrazanetti
PhD in Architecture, she lectures and researches at the Department of Architecture and Urban Studies at the Politecnico di Milano. She works as independent curator on exhibitions and publishing projects, writing on architecture, design and theatre. She is editor of the magazine 'Stratagemmi'.

Matteo Schubert
Director of the culture department of ABCittà s.c.r.l. and the architecture firm Alterstudio Partners srl, with which he has carried out numerous cultural and architectural projects for private and public sector clients, winning national and international awards. He has developed and curated various events, exhibitions and publications.

Other authors:

Ciro Najle
Architect, researcher, educator, Dean at the School of Architecture and UrbanStudies at the Universidad Torcuato Di Tella, Visiting Professor at the Harvard University Graduate School of Design, co-founder and former Director of the Landscape Urbanism Graduate Design Master Program and Diploma Unit Master at the Architectural Association. He has taught at various universities.
Director of GDB General Design Bureau, curator of the London Pavilion at he Beijing Biennale of Architecture 2004, his work has been exhibited internationally.

Hugo Mondragón L.
He is associate professor at the School of Architecture of the Pontifical Catholic University of Chile (UC) where he alternates between teaching and research.
He received the professional degree of architect at the Piloto University of Colombia in 1990. He was awarded the degrees of Master in Theory and History of Art and Architecture (2003) at the National University of Colombia. He is also Master in Architecture (2002) and Doctor in Architecture and Urban Studies (2010) at the Pontifical Catholic University of Chile.

Collaborators:

Mariana Bravo, Maria Mazzanti, Carlos Medellín, Saskia Rachello.

The credits of the photographs reproduced in this volume are:

pp. 142-143: Rodrigo Dávila